The Golden Years

THE SIEGAL-MARGOLIS DOG LIBRARY

The Golden Years

A Pet Owner's Guide to the Golden Retriever

BY

MORDECAI SIEGAL

and

MATTHEW MARGOLIS

Photographs by Karen Taylor

LITTLE, BROWN AND COMPANY Boston New York Toronto London

First Edition

The authors are grateful for permission to include the following previously copyrighted material:

Excerpts from *Official Standard for the Golden Retriever*, adopted by the Golden Retriever Club of America. Copyright © 1991 by the American Kennel Club, Inc. Reprinted by permission of the American Kennel Club, Inc.

Excerpts from *A Guide To Dog Schools* by Ed and Toni Eames. Copyright © 1994 by Ed and Toni Eames. Reprinted by permission of the authors.

All photographs used with the permission of Karen Taylor, with the following exceptions: pp. 38–39 used with the permission of Mordecai Siegal; p. 52 used with the permission of Karen Newcombe.

Library of Congress Cataloging-in-Publication Data

Siegal, Mordecai.
    The golden years : a pet owner's guide to the golden retriever / by Mordecai Siegal and Matthew Margolis ; photographs by Karen Taylor. — 1st ed.
        p.   cm.
    "The Siegal-Margolis dog library."
    ISBN 0-316-79017-6
    1. Golden retrievers.   I. Margolis, Matthew.   II. Title.
SF429.G63S56   1996
636.7'52 — dc20   96-5223

10 9 8 7 6 5 4 3 2 1

RRD-IN

Published simultaneously in Canada by Little, Brown & Company (Canada) Limited

Printed in the United States of America

THIS BOOK

IS LOVINGLY DEDICATED TO

Sherry Davis and her Golden boys, Timmy and Bruce

Contents

Acknowledgments

We are deeply indebted to Sherry Davis for generously blessing this book with her knowledge of, experience with, and feelings for the Golden Retriever. Throughout the writing of this book she was a wellspring of insights and information for us. Her love for Golden Retrievers and her understanding of the breed is reflected throughout. We are grateful. Sherry Davis is a breeder, exhibitor, and consummate dog trainer. Her life revolves around her own dogs and those entrusted to her. She is the Executive Director of Training for the National Institute of Dog Training in Los Angeles.

Janel Wilson provided all of the research for the canine health chapters, especially the medical conditions and disorders all dog owners need to know about. Her energy and devotion to the task made it possible to present the essential veterinary information that specifically applies to Golden Retrievers. She unearthed a mountain of veterinary science concerning the good, the bad, and the incurable. She gave us much more information than a book of this scope permits. Nevertheless, there is a surprisingly extravagant content of medical information for the Golden Retriever owner offered within these pages. We thank her most profoundly for her major contribution. Janel Wilson is the Director of Canine Health at the National Institute of Dog Training in Los Angeles.

We are completely indebted to animal photographer Karen Taylor for her sumptuous photographs of the Golden Retriever and the world it inhabits which are displayed on these pages. Her gorgeous photographs in this book have made learning about the Golden Retriever an enjoyable experience for the authors as well as for the readers. We have been able to broaden our knowledge and appreciation of the breed from this fine photographer's exceptional work. Ms. Taylor can be found in Taylor, Michigan, which is another source of wonder for us. Not many photographers have a town named for them.

Many dogs and their owners allowed us to use their glorious images, and for that we are very grateful. We take this opportunity to acknowledge their kind and generous cooperation. Please see About the Photographs, page 201, for their names.

We are especially pleased to add a warm thank you to Ed and Toni Eames for suggesting to us the idea of Guide Dog schools as a source of Golden Retriever pets. It was also their fine suggestion that we reprint a small portion of their publication *A Guide to Guide Dog Schools*. It was an added treat to include a photo of these two blind educators and writers and their dogs, Jake and Escort (Goldens, of course). Ed and Toni Eames are an inspiration for all who are lucky enough to meet them. The photograph was taken by Karen Newcombe.

There is no better source of information about Golden Retrievers than those who breed, handle, and live with them every day of their lives. We prepared an extensive questionnaire and sent it out to a number of top Golden people. Those acknowledged here very willingly answered our questions beyond our expectations and thus added much to the validity of this book. Those who responded did so in order to give novice Golden Retriever owners the benefit of their experience and knowledge. Many of their answers to our questions confirmed what we had already perceived to be true. However, there were many new insights offered and they were gratefully accepted. Here then are the names of those Golden Retriever breeders and serious owners who are quoted in this book: Paul and Sue Dougherty, Briarwood Farms, Uxbridge, Massachusetts; Jim and Debbie Berry, Sunshine Golden Retrievers, Dexter, Oregon; Karen B. Fennikoh,

Amberglo Goldens, Goshen, New York; Susan Jaffe, Bronxville, New York; Robert Crowley, Mt. Airy, Maryland; Amanda L. Dorner, Hyline Golden Retrievers, Hartland, Wisconsin; Tom and Jocelyn Lewis, Dublin, California; Debi Hanson, Sherwood Golden Retrievers, San Bruno, California.

Introduction

As you read this sentence, your lovable Golden Retriever is probably turning his water bowl upside down and splashing in the puddles with his large paws. He expects you to be as excited to see him and his puddles as he is to see you the minute you walk in the door. Your very presence makes him happy. He brings you his ball and invites you to play with him as he smiles with his slurping tongue. But if something is seriously wrong and you feel bad, your Golden senses it right away and is likely to console you by gently giving you his paw or by laying his head on your lap. He gladly shares your sadness as well as your happiness. A Golden Retriever is a special breed of dog and deserves the best care you can give him. That is the purpose of this book.

The Golden Years will help you understand the breed you have chosen to live with. It tells you how to keep your Golden healthy and how to train him with love and kindness. The authors suggest you read this book as soon as possible, after cleaning the kitchen floor, of course.

The Golden Years is a *how-to* book for pet owners, especially for those who are inexperienced with the breed. It is sharply focused on the breed's temperament, personality, health needs, health problems, and response to basic obedience training. Offered within these pages is a complete basic dog training course formulated specifically for the Golden Retriever.

If you are about to acquire a Golden Retriever or if you have recently brought one into your life, then you know that there isn't a cuter puppy face on the planet. You are quite likely aware that a Golden Retriever always brings a smile to your face, whether you are an outgoing or reserved person. Nevertheless, there are many important things you need to know if you are to develop a happy, loving relationship with your dog. For example, training a Golden Retriever is not difficult; the breed's desire to please makes it easy. But Goldens are sensitive dogs, and training techniques for this breed must be tailored to their temperament. They are star students who can be poetry in motion when handled properly.

The Golden Years is a user-friendly owner's guide and hands-on manual loaded with essential information and insights into this delightful dog breed.

The Golden Years

Meet the Golden Retriever

You are about to enter your Golden years and your life will never be the same again. Just one glance into the chocolate eyes of these, the most lovable dogs on earth, and your heart will stir, stirring emotions through your body like soft electricity. These gentle dogs are playful, funny, and irresistibly huggable. They trot out of your fantasies and noisily leap into real life. Golden Retrievers are living proof that dreams do come true. It is impossible to keep your hands off these stand-up comedians. At times they are uninhibited clowns, and at other times they are the essence of canine dignity. To know them is to love them. Meet the Golden Retriever.

The Breed in Profile

A breed profile will help you make the right decision if you are considering living with a Golden Retriever. In the event that you have already brought one home, it will be even more useful, by helping you understand the newest member of your family.

The first thing a family wants to know when deciding on a dog is what he is going to be like. Will he love you and be your friend? Will he fit into your lifestyle? Will he be fun to be with? Or will he just pee on the wallpaper, dig up the azalea bushes, and nip the UPS driver because he doesn't like his uniform? If you are in the process of choosing a dog, the primary consideration must be behavior. What will your dog be like? It's a big question.

All dogs share a common set of fundamental behaviors designed to help them reproduce and survive that can be seen in every aspect of their lives. Each breed, however, has behaviors that may be exaggerated, diminished, or unique to that breed. These behavioral variations are what make most dog breeds different from each other, in addition to their physical distinctions. They are predictable enough to give new dog owners a fairly accurate idea of what they should expect from a dog of a particular breed. Of course, each dog has its own personality differences, and these are less predictable. Nevertheless, it is helpful to learn in advance about the breed you are interested in.

The Golden Retriever's Original Function

To better understand your new dog's behavior, you should begin by learning about the breed's original function. This will help you understand your dog's traits and behaviors, because most of them are linked to it. Almost every breed has been established by serious people who have selected dogs for mating to emphasize size, type, coat, sensory abilities, skills, or behaviors. The 400 breeds (more or less) throughout the world are largely the result of human intervention in the mating process. Most breeds were created in order to develop dogs that were useful to humans in special environments and jobs, such as herding, guarding, various aspects of hunting, and in many other practical tasks.

The original function of Golden Retrievers was to assist hunters in the taking of waterfowl and upland game birds. Their job was to locate and retrieve birds that were shot by hunters. Although their

skills are well suited for upland game birds that hide in the brush, such as pheasant, quail, and doves, Golden Retrievers are most useful to hunters of wild duck, geese, and assorted waterfowl. This is mostly because of the retriever's exceptional ability to swim, especially with a bird in its mouth.

In the early part of the nineteenth century, English bird hunters began developing dogs that would locate fallen game and retrieve it without damaging it with their teeth. These dogs were also bred to refrain from hunting for live game, as Spaniels did during that time. Thus began the development of the early Retriever types out of which has come the Golden Retriever.

A typical field-working Golden Retriever, if trained properly, will sit quietly with a hunter in a duck blind without giving away their presence. If the dog is allowed to watch through a peephole as the hunter shoots, he can visually "mark" where each bird falls, even from a great distance. Like most Retrievers, he will remember the locations. On command, the dog will dash out of the duck blind, plunge into icy-cold water, and swim quickly to the fallen bird. Like an Olympian, the dog will swim back to shore with the undamaged bird in its "soft mouth" to present the prize to the hunter. If required, the dog will go back into the water for other fallen birds. It is what he was born to do.

Golden Retrievers have been bred from their earliest beginnings for their intelligence, pleasing disposition, and even temperament, qualities that have blended well with their abilities in the field. However, the great majority of Goldens today are pets, show dogs, or service dogs. Only a relatively few work at the hunter's side despite the fact that their natural skills and inclinations for fieldwork remain as part of their personalities.

Golden Retriever Temperament

Golden Retrievers love people and are pleasing companions. They are born with a gentle, adaptive nature that allows them to live happily with most people in most homes. It is their easygoing nature that has created the desire in so many pet owners to bring them into their home as part of their family.

Typical Goldens are eager, alert, and self-confident. They are high-energy dogs that are ready to join in any activity you have in mind whenever you say the word. As high-energy dogs, they enjoy physical activities and never resist participating in them, nor do they unwillingly drag through various forms of work. They love games and going for walks.

Most Goldens are alert, eager, and self-confident.

Energetic Golden Retrievers should not be mistaken for *hyperactive* dogs. Hyperactive dogs are nervous, cannot sit still, are never comfortable, and never feel relaxed in their situation. Despite their abundance of enthusiasm, Goldens, by contrast, are perfectly capable of relaxing and spending time quietly, especially if the time is shared with a member of the family. Of course, a Golden will be ready for any activity you have in mind in an instant.

Golden Retrievers are responsive dogs. They accept training well and have an engaging desire to please. Those who live with them never hesitate to tell anyone how their dog tenderly responds to the concerns of its family. When Goldens look at you, their eyes reflect your feelings with unusual accuracy. They only seem to be human.

As a breed, Goldens are sensitive but not shy. Shy dogs are frightened, easily intimidated, and defensively aggressive. Sensitive dogs simply want your approval and cannot bear a bad-tempered rejection. A stern tone of voice is all that is necessary as a reprimand.

Even that much produces a hurt look. This is not a breed that can tolerate harsh treatment or physical punishment of any kind. Goldens want to please you, and when they foul up it is usually because they were trying too hard.

Living with Your Golden Retriever

The first year with Golden Retrievers is pure pleasure because they are high-energy dogs and fun to be with. Goldens are ready for anything; all you have to do is say the word. They see people: they like people. They want people to see them and to like them. Typically, they cannot wait to get into the family car with you. They will be ready to go before you are. They are always by your side and want to be part of what you are doing. This is in contrast to hyperactive dogs that are not fun, that have to be constantly corrected, that are always moving, always panting, always uncomfortable.

Golden owners soon discover they can release their dog's boundless energy by working him with training sessions, exercise, or play. Tossing a ball or stick and having the dog retrieve gives supreme pleasure to these dogs and uses up much of their energy. A vigorous swim is what they love most. Puppies, having much more energy than adult dogs, have less control of their enthusiasm, but this changes with maturity. These are dogs that are eager to learn and exceptionally bright.

Goldens can be taught almost anything. Ironically, if you unintentionally teach them a negative behavior, they will remember it and use it to get you to look at them or play with them. If a Golden puppy steals your underwear and you laugh, he will continue to do it for years, waiting for the reward of your laughter. These things become attention-getters to make you hang up the phone or stop talking to a friend and look at the dog.

As the years pass, you will discover that an important part of Goldens' charm is their quick emotional transition from exuberant play to attentive concern for you. A Golden is quite likely at some unsuspecting moment to lay his head on your arm and look into your eyes with unbelievable sensitivity. These are dogs full of surprises.

Important breed traits of the Golden Retriever are their love of people, their desire to get along with other dogs, their need to be cared for (including bathing, brushing, training), their constantly wanting to be petted, and their carrying anything and everything in their mouth. They love food and live for their next meal; they will do what they must to get it. They are very responsive to all forms of training. They can be taught to go hiking with you, to perform well in obedience trials, to behave appropriately with hospital patients, to work as therapy and assistance dogs. There is little they cannot be taught to do except work as protection dogs.

There is more to owning a Golden than the attention *you* give to the dog. You must be willing to accept all the attention that will be given to your dog; almost everyone who sees him will admire him and want to pet such a handsome dog. You will be unable to walk down the street without attracting those who want to stop you and look at your very special dog.

Goldens have a technique for getting you to hold, hug, and pet them. They come up under your arm with their head, nudge it upward, and flick your arm in the air so that it will drop over the back of their neck. This causes the palm of your hand to land flat on the dog's back. All Goldens do it.

Goldens can melt your heart with a look and get anything they want from you. A wistful stare usually means "Feed me."

Golden Retrievers know they are beautiful and never let you forget it. They are always posing. After you brush them, they tend to parade around and let you express your admiration. This behavior is reinforced by the frequency with which people tell them how beautiful they are.

An important breed trait is their intense desire to be with their family as much as possible. Nothing pleases them more than being in the backyard and having you toss a ball for them. However, if you go inside, they want to go in with you. Goldens are among the most social of all dogs and want the company of you, your friends, your neighbors, and anyone else who comes to visit. They are good-time dogs.

An important reason for the great popularity of Goldens is their ability to withstand city stress. They are among the most adaptive of all dogs, adjusting easily to family life after dog shows, obedience trials, or even fieldwork, and they love every minute of the transition. They are the perfect dog to grow old with.

Golden Retrievers have only a few inherent negative traits. They shed seasonally. If they are not brushed at least once a week, their fur gets on everything. They may scratch themselves excessively, creating skin irritations, or "hot spots." Thorough brushing several times a week controls the problem.

A laughable but annoying trait is their love of playing with their water bowl and sloshing around the floor in puddles they created. Some Goldens enjoy slurping a drink and bringing it to you in their mouth, no matter what you are wearing. Almost all of these dogs will sooner or later dunk their toys in the water bowl and bring them to you dripping wet. Golden Retrievers are not ideal dogs for exceptionally neat and tidy people, but their messiness may be tolerated by those who love the breed and may not necessarily be considered negative by everyone. Of course, negative traits that are not typical of the breed can be less than endearing.

What the Breeders Say

In a questionnaire sent to a number of active Golden Retriever breeders, they were asked to describe the typical personality traits of the breed. It is interesting to see how many of them agree with each other and offer similar comments. These are their responses:

> *"Golden Retrievers have a deep yearning to be with people. Their whole quest in life is to be loved and to play, to please you. They are very intelligent and enjoy being the class clown one minute and dignified the next.*

When your Golden looks up into your face as only this breed can do, you will experience what complete love and adoration is."

"A Golden Retriever should be friendly, confident, and able to play happily outside and be able to settle down inside and be a good member of the household."

"[They are] loyal, willing to please, intelligent, even-tempered, moderately active as puppies, more laid-back as adults, sweet and loving and an ideal family dog, and they are wonderful with children."

"*Warm, friendly, sweet, fun-loving, amiable, trainable, and sometimes bright.*"

"*Very friendly, well-tempered — a well-bred Golden is fairly low-key, but happy to cooperate in any activity you choose. Very people-oriented. Easy to train, eager to please. Stoic. Oral-oriented. Gentle and loving.*"

"*A happy, positive dog, believing the best of everyone. Usually a ball or toy in the mouth is a given [for play]. Some 'talk' with enthusiasm. Fear should not be part of the personality, as in spookiness, etc. They are perennial puppies; even old and gray they love to play.*"

"*Kind, loving, even-tempered, a true companion and 'best friend.' The breed standard mentions alertness and self-confidence.*"

"*Friendly, outgoing, intelligent, love people and children. Love other dogs.*"

The breeders were also asked, "What behavioral characteristics are unique to your breed?" They answered:

"*Puppies: Energetic, curious, learn quickly. They love to carry things around. They are very vocal.*"

"*Adults: Same.*"

"*Golden Retrievers are very mouthy and therefore tend to carry things around in their mouth most of the time. If you do not provide them with acceptable items to carry, they will search for anything that fulfills that desire. We do not discourage this trait; instead we give them safe items. While supervised: stuffed toys with ribbons, eyes, etc. removed; balls of different sizes and textures; latex squeak toys; rope tug toys; compressed rawhide bones. No supervision: balls, Kong toys, sterilized bones and Nylabones in large sizes. On the whole, they tend to be rather quiet and do not make very good guard dogs. They should be happy and trustworthy and not fearful of strangers. Since they love the water, if you have a pool or any other body of water, special care should be taken to guarantee their safety.*"

"Puppies: Puppies are usually active and quite inquisitive. Like most retrievers, socks, shoes and other personal and household items are fair game. They also seek a great deal of attention and are so darn cute, they usually get it. That is why they are seen in so many ads and TV commercials.

"Adults: Large puppies. They still seek human companionship and attention. Young adults are quite active, and most are very trainable. In the later years, they never lose the desire to be close to humans."

"As puppies: G.R.'s are great 'talkers'; they like to get a toy or ball in their mouth and walk around saying, 'Woo-woo.' If you've ever owned one, you will know this.

"As adults: G.R.'s are easily the most friendly breed alive. They love everyone."

"Puppies: Like to chew (oral-oriented) a great deal.

"Adults: Like, need to be with people."

"As puppies: Mouth-oriented, many 'talk' strange groaning sounds of joy. Can develop chewing vice if not supervised.

"As adults: Same. Some become ball maniacs, obsessed, easy to exercise."

"Puppies: Besides being cute they are outgoing, very eager to learn, very responsive, playing and exploring all the time.

"Adults: Intelligent, outgoing, calm when needed, up and responsive when requested. Nonaggressive."

Nontypical Traits

It is important to understand that some dogs are *not* typical of their breed and create a false impression about breed characteristics. Occasionally a Golden is born that is not typical and can only be considered a genetic misfortune. This has happened to most breeders at one time or another despite their experience and good intentions.

However, *most* dogs that are not typical of their breed are the result of bad breeding practices. Bad examples of the breed are most often the result of ignorance, apathy, the irresponsible pursuit of profit, and greed. When a breed becomes as popular as the Golden Retriever, it is always in danger of being exploited in an attempt to satisfy the great demand by overbreeding.

The law of supply and demand motivates profiteers to mate all the Golden Retrievers they can get their hands on without the selectivity necessary for a good breeding program. In that situation there is no thought of the health or behavior of the dogs that are mated. Dogs that may have inherited diseases, disorders, poor breed type or temperament are most likely going to pass on those negative factors to their puppies. Once atypical breed traits or health problems are established in the gene pool, it is anyone's guess which future puppies will inherit those problems.

Other reasons for atypical breed traits that appear in Goldens may be harmful circumstances and events that have occurred in the dog's life. Among these could have been harsh and unhealthy living conditions, abusive treatment, no training, improper training, little or no medical attention, isolation from people, or serious mistakes made by uninformed breeders or dog owners.

What the Breeders Say

Breeders of Golden Retrievers were also asked in the questionnaire, "Which traits would be *atypical* of the breed?" Once again there is much agreement among them. Here are their replies:

"Shyness, indifference, and a lack of interest in life."

"A Golden Retriever should never be fearful or tuck his tail, shy away from people or other dogs. He should never act aggressively toward other dogs or people, although he may protect his home."

"Any aggression, aloof, hyperactive, uninterested in activities going on about it and, in general, anything contrary."

"Aggressive, nervous, protective, stubborn."

"Aggressiveness, hyperactive, loners, one-man dogs."

"Unfortunately, many Goldens end up too calm and/or too coddled by their owners and are, therefore, 'wimpy,' or easily intimidated by unfamiliar people and/or places."

"Aggressive. Shy. Not friendly with others or people."

Searching for a Golden Retriever Puppy

Selecting the best Golden Retriever for you and your family requires some homework and some legwork. Read as much as possible about the breed (in books, articles, pamphlets) and then go out and meet the Golden people (exhibitors, breeders, veterinarians, dog trainers, groomers, pet owners) and talk to them, asking them all the questions you can think of. These activities are not only interesting and informative, they are also great fun. If you do this, you will become capable of selecting the best puppy available. You will also be quite proud of yourself and your new dog.

Although dogs are everywhere and getting one is easy, getting the *right* one is a little harder. Acquiring a dog on impulse can be a disaster waiting to happen. Some people become pet owners by chance. This may happen when a puppy is purchased as a last-minute Christmas or birthday gift or if you give in to the emotional appeal of a young puppy cunningly placed in your arms. Getting a dog in such a way often leads to anger and sadness. Of course, many people have successfully found pet dogs without much fuss and have been very happy with the outcome. Nevertheless, the risk of failure is high, and it can lead to heartbreak for everyone concerned. The best chance of avoiding this is to learn how to select a sound, healthy dog.

Before selecting a puppy, attend All-Breed or Specialty dog shows featuring the Golden Retriever. Show listings can be obtained directly from the American Kennel Club, the United Kennel Club, or from the Golden Retriever Club of America. This will give you an opportunity to see good examples of the breed and talk to owners, handlers, and breeders. At a dog show you will definitely find many sources for high-quality Golden Retrievers. You can also find breeder ads in the popular dog magazines such as *Dogs USA, Dog Fancy, AKC Gazette, Dog World,* or in *Blood Lines* (UKC). Write or call the American Kennel Club for their breeder referral information or for the address of the current secretary of the Golden Retriever Club of America, from whom you can obtain a list of Golden Retriever breeders in your region. Write to: American Kennel Club, 51 Madison Avenue, New York, New York 10010.

Selecting a Good Puppy

Puppies are appealing and huggable. On first sight you will want to take them all home because it is difficult to choose one over the other. Their large brown eyes seem to say, "Take me. I love you." Golden puppies are tantalizing and make it almost impossible to make an intelligent selection. Apart from noting personality differences and which one looks best, the most important criteria for selecting a pet dog are health and temperament. It is in your best interest to know the difference between a puppy that is healthy and of good temperament from one that is not.

Most breeders proudly show likely buyers a pedigree, which is an impressive-looking document outlining a puppy's parentage, or family tree, going back at least three generations. It will tell you a lot about a puppy if you are familiar with Golden Retrievers of high quality by name and with the kennels that produced them. It is a meaningless document to those who know little or nothing about such matters as "foundation stock," past and present Golden Retriever champions, and the kennels that produced the dogs mentioned in the pedigree.

However, most breeders are eager to explain a puppy's pedigree to you if you show the slightest interest. There is something to be gained by reading the document even if you don't understand all of

If you do your homework, it won't be hard to find a healthy, good-tempered puppy.

it. For example, if there is at least one dog listed in the pedigree with a *Champion* title, it is an indication that the puppy comes from a line of quality breeding. Of course, you may still get a great dog with or without a champion in the family tree, especially if it is to be a companion animal. If you have done your homework, you will be able to recognize a few of the names of the kennels with important reputations. One could very easily show up on a pedigree.

Another important document a breeder or retailer may show you is an AKC registration certificate for the litter of puppies you are looking at or for an individual puppy. *An official American Kennel Club or United Kennel Club registration certificate is a document that is supposed to prove a dog's purebred status. That is all it means. It does not guarantee in any way the quality of a dog or puppy. It is important to understand this.*

It is far more useful to see the mother or father of the puppies you are looking at. One or the other should be available if you are visiting a kennel. This is where your experience at dog shows and the books and pictures you have examined will serve you. If the puppies' parents appear to be in good health and seem to have an even temperament, it is likely that their puppies will grow to be somewhat like their parents. If you have read the *Official Standard for the Golden Retriever* from the American Kennel Club (reprinted at the end of this chapter), you should be able to tell if the dogs come close to it or not.

Because most puppies are bought as companion animals, a breeder may refer you to a "pet quality" dog rather than one with "show potential." Do not be put off by this. Many breeders will not sell a puppy with show potential to someone who wants a pet. Those puppies are usually reserved for the breeder if he or she shows dogs or for someone who will "campaign" them at dog shows and try to win the fifteen points necessary for a Champion title. This is an expensive and time-consuming activity. Dogs that earn the title Champion help establish a kennel's reputation and the quality of its breeding program. For the breeder it is a matter of pride and economics.

"Pet quality" puppies are wonderful dogs. Important matters of health and temperament are different considerations from a puppy's "show potential." Such dogs have simply not met every aspect of the Official Standard and have limited chances for winning dog shows, which should not matter to anyone who just wants a dog to live with. Pet quality dogs are the best companion animals in the world.

Choosing a Healthy Puppy

The most important consideration when selecting a puppy is good health. A simple set of observations when looking at a litter of puppies or an individual dog will help enormously. It is essential to be as objective as possible and try to discover any medical problems *before* you make your selection. Nothing short of a veterinary examination can accurately reveal all aspects of a puppy's health. You are entirely on your own when making your puppy selection.

Still, you do not have to be a health-care professional to know when you are looking at puppies in good health. A healthy litter of puppies should be frisky and outgoing; they should appear to be enjoying themselves and glow with good health. If there is one puppy in the group that is sluggish, upset-looking, walks or runs with a limp, has an exceptionally unhealthy-looking coat, or shows any obvious signs of bad health, be cautious about your selection.

The coat

The puppy coat should be soft, bright, and healthy-looking without clumps, mats, or bald patches. A coat in bad condition can be a sign of disease, parasites (worms, fleas, ticks, etc.), physical stress, emotional stress, or an unhealthy environment. A healthy puppy's coat should be loose, supple, and have no bald patches of hair or dandruff-like flakes. At a very young age it is normal for the Golden coat to be somewhat fluffy and without a lot of shine.

The skin

The skin underneath should not have any damaged surfaces, scaly areas, or sores. A puppy's skin or haircoat should not show evidence of fleas, which resembles grains of salt and pepper. Active fleas may or may not be visible. Your new puppy should have clean, smooth, undamaged skin.

The eyes

Healthy eyes should be clear, clean, and alert, with no excessive watering or sensitivity to light. Unnatural markings or inconsistent coloring on the corneas (the outer covering of the eye) may indicate corneal ulcers, which appear as colorless, indented spots. They are considered to be a serious medical condition. If a puppy's eyes seem to tear excessively or if he continually rubs his eyes with a paw, he probably has a medical problem.

The ears

The ears of a Golden Retriever puppy should be clean, particularly on the inner surface. Dirty-looking or waxy material inside may mean the puppy has ear mites. Ear mites are minute white specks that move. They are common parasites in dogs and cause infection. If a puppy shakes its head excessively, scratches and rubs its ears, and behaves in a restless manner, it is very likely infected with mites. Veterinary care is necessary.

To test for deafness, slap your hands behind a puppy's ears. Rattle some keys loudly where he cannot see them. If there is no response, it is likely the puppy does not have normal hearing.

Choosing a Puppy with a Good Temperament

When selecting a puppy, temperament is one of the most important aspects to consider. This has an important bearing on emotional stability and the potential for acceptable behavior as an adult dog. A Golden Retriever puppy that is going to be a companion animal should be playful, enthusiastic, curious, eager, self-confident, energetic, and affectionate. Do not look for the most pushy puppy unless you are looking for a show prospect; in that case choose the boldest puppy of the litter. That dog will want people to pay attention to him and that kind of behavior is best for the show ring.

What is unique to Goldens is the way they shower you with a million kisses. Golden puppies should come right up to you and lick your face. Normal puppies love everybody. If one puppy in a litter is described as "calm," it is a substitution for the word *shy*. Normal Goldens do not become truly calm until they are three years old. This is true of most breeds. All puppies should be active and all over the place; if not, something is wrong.

Beware of shy, timid, or overly aggressive puppies. What is heartwarming or cute at twelve weeks can make you quite unhappy at six or eight months of age. A shy puppy may cringe, cower, or become aggressive when petted, picked up, or cornered in any way. Golden puppies that are not curious, energetic, playful, or anxious to greet you are either sick or untypical of the breed and should be avoided. (Of course, puppies can also be tired at the time of viewing and may simply want to take a nap.) When considering buying a puppy, try to imagine what he will be like as a grown dog. Look for an outgoing, friendly dog who comes right up to you and does not hide in the corner or run with fear.

Do not choose a puppy with a *shy* temperament. Shy dogs grow up to be abnormally frightened of anyone or anything that is unfamiliar. They do their best to avoid most people, animals, or changes in their environment.

A puppy with a mild temperament is not necessarily a *shy* puppy. A mild-tempered puppy may be somewhat aloof with strangers and take a wait-and-see attitude before making direct contact. That is not the same as shyness, which is a serious behavior deficiency.

Another temperament type to avoid is the *aggressive* dog. Puppies that growl seriously from their throat are warning you that they will bite. That is unacceptable and undesirable behavior and indicative of an aggressive puppy who will grow into an aggressive, possibly dangerous dog. If you are suspicious of overly aggressive behavior, place the puppy on his back and hold him with your hand placed on his neck for ten or fifteen seconds. A puppy with a potential behavior problem will growl, snarl, howl, bark, and even snap and bite to get back on his feet. Do not choose this puppy as a pet.

Puppies that have been handled by humans on a regular basis after three weeks of age have been "socialized." This means they will be more adaptable to living with humans and will accept obedience training easily. If they have been allowed to remain with their mother and litter mates for seven weeks, they are likely to adjust easily to other dogs as well as humans (providing they have been socialized).

The transference of genetic characteristics plays an important role in dog behavior, too. If the puppies' mother and father are at ease with strangers, congenial, outgoing, and friendly, it is likely that their puppies will be the same, providing they have been handled properly.

When observing a litter of puppies, kneel at floor level and observe which ones are curious about you, friendly toward you, want you to touch them. With the breeder's permission, lift them in your arms, one at a time, to see if they are at ease with you. Hold each puppy in your arms with the belly facing up. If the dog submits with ease and pleasure, his temperament is just fine. If he squirms desperately to get away, he may be aggressive or nervous. If he whines and whimpers, he may be shy. A normal puppy will either thrash about playfully or settle in and enjoy the contact. He should follow you around when you set him down on the floor. Try playing with him. A friendly, outgoing puppy should enjoy playing with you. He may roll on his back and flail his paws in the air or place your finger in his mouth or try to climb on you and lick your face.

Try tossing something for the puppies to retrieve. They should respond well to this. Get them to come to you by clapping your hands. Observe how social they are with each other. Pay attention to whether or not they interact reasonably with their brothers and sisters. Avoid a loner or a puppy that is a bully around the food or in play.

A new puppy should be taken to his new home at eight weeks of age. This makes bonding with the young dog more successful. Waiting longer than eight weeks makes the process more difficult unless the puppy has interacted with many different people. See Chapter 4, "The Golden Bond." There is more to canine health than clear eyes and a glossy coat. A happy, self-assured puppy that delights in the company of humans is likely to enjoy good health and long life.

The Official Golden Retriever

Serious breeders and exhibitors (those who compete at dog shows) work hard to produce dogs that compare favorably to the American Kennel Club's Official Standard for their breed. This is not only appropriate but essential, because these are members of the *Dog Fancy* who have the responsibility of preserving (and improving) the qualities of their breed, which include physical characteristics and behavioral traits.

Although pet owners rarely have the same concerns about their dogs as breeders and exhibitors, some considerations apply equally when selecting a good dog. Many potential pet owners are not sure what the breed of choice should actually look like or what kind of behavior to expect. Attending canine competitions (the *dog sport*) involving obedience trials, field trials, hunting tests, agility, and other contests may be helpful, but the most popular event is the dog show. The dog show, as sanctioned by the American Kennel Club, is formally referred to as a *conformation show*. It is a competition concerned with a dog's skeletal form, musculature, movement and gait, coat color and pattern, and overall appearance, health, and behavior.

In a dog show the dogs' various physical structures are judged against guidelines detailed in the Official Standard. It is not a beauty contest, although many dogs entered in dog shows are among the most beautiful-looking in the world. The "conformation" of a dog pertains to overall appearance and physical formation, involving both its individual characteristics and the sum total of those characteristics as a well-balanced composite.

American Kennel Club judges examine each dog in competition and decide how closely it compares to the descriptions in the Official Standard for the breed. The dogs that are judged to be closest to the

written standard win points for a championship title (fifteen required), awards, and prizes. Although the Official Standard for any breed represents an ideal, it is used by breeders, exhibitors, and show judges as an important guideline for evaluating dogs within a breed.

It is worth the effort for potential pet owners to read the Official Standard of the breed of dog they want. How else can you determine if the puppy being considered comes close to the type of dog you have your heart set on? Before you read the standard, however, here are a few pointers that can be of help with the puppy selection.

Size

Although the standard offers a category of "Size, Proportion, Substance," the pet owner should not allow a puppy's size to become an issue. Often, the smallest Golden puppy grows to be a big dog. A puppy's size is not necessarily an indication of its height or weight as an adult dog. Look for an average-size puppy somewhere in the middle when compared to the others in the litter, not the largest, not the smallest.

Coat color

All shades of the rich, golden hair color are acceptable in the show ring and should be considered by the pet owner. The consideration of coat color is a matter of personal preference (and puppy availability) and does not reflect negatively on breed type. The colors range from deep red to yellow-gold to cream. Many Goldens have an allowable dot of white hair on the chest, which is common and is not penalized in the show ring. Some puppies have dark skin pigmentation on the stomach, beneath the coat, which often lightens or disappears with maturity. No acceptable Golden Retriever has any black hairs in the coat. Some experts believe that the color of the hair on a puppy's ears indicates what the color will be when the dog is an adult.

Eyes

A Golden Retriever puppy that is true to type should have dark brown eyes, the darker the better. The eyes should always be darker than the coat color.

Official breed standards are created by the various national breed clubs and reviewed and approved by the American Kennel Club.

With that in mind and with the generous permission of the American Kennel Club, we reprint here the *Official Standard for the Golden Retriever*.

Official Standard for the
GOLDEN RETRIEVER

(adopted by the Golden Retriever Club of America and approved by The American Kennel Club, Inc.)

General Appearance—A symmetrical, powerful, active dog, sound and well put together, not clumsy nor long in the leg, displaying a kindly expression and possessing a personality that is eager, alert and self-confident. Primarily a hunting dog, he should be shown in hard working condition. Overall appearance, balance, gait and purpose to be given more emphasis than any of his component parts.

Faults—Any departure from the described ideal shall be considered faulty to the degree to which it interferes with the breed's purpose or is contrary to breed character.

Size, Proportion, Substance—Males 23–24 inches in height at withers; females 21½–22½ inches. Dogs up to one inch above or below standard size should be proportionately penalized. Deviation in height of more than one inch from the standard shall *disqualify*.

Length from breastbone to point of buttocks slightly greater than height at withers in ration of 12:11. Weight for dogs 65–75 pounds; bitches 55–65 pounds.

Head—Broad in **skull**, slightly arched laterally and longitudinally without prominence of frontal bones (forehead) or occipital bones. *Stop* well defined but not abrupt. *Foreface* deep and wide, nearly as long as skull. **Muzzle** straight in profile, blend-

The American Kennel Club's Official Standard for the Golden Retriever *calls for a symmetrical, powerful dog with a friendly and intelligent expression.*

ing smooth and strongly into skull; when viewed in profile or from above, slightly deeper and wider at stop than at tip. No heaviness in flews. Removal of whiskers is permitted but not preferred.

Eyes friendly and intelligent in expression, medium large with dark, close-fitting rims, set well apart and reasonably deep in sockets. Color preferably dark brown; medium brown acceptable. Slant eyes and narrow, triangular eyes detract from correct expression and are to be faulted. No white or haw visible when looking straight ahead. Dogs showing evidence of functional abnormality of eyelids or eyelashes (such as, but not limited to, trichiasis, entropion, ectropion, or distichiasis) are to be excused from the ring.

Ears rather short with front edge attached well behind and just above the eye and falling close to cheek. When pulled forward, tip of ear should just cover the eye. Low, hound-like ear set to be faulted.

Nose black or brownish black, though fading to a lighter shade in cold weather not serious. Pink nose or one seriously lacking in pigmentation to be faulted.

Teeth scissors bite, in which the outer side of the lower incisors touches the inner side of the upper incisors. Misalignment of teeth (irregular placement of incisors) or a level bite (incisors meet each other edge to edge) is undesirable, but not to be confused with undershot or overshot. Full dentition. Obvious gaps are serious faults.

Neck, Topline, Body — Neck medium long, merging gradually into well laid back shoulders, giving sturdy, muscular appearance. No throatiness.

Backline strong and level from withers to slightly sloping croup, whether standing or moving. Sloping backline, roach or sway back, flat or steep croup to be faulted.

Body well balanced, short coupled, deep through the chest. *Chest* between forelegs at least as wide as a man's closed hand including thumb, with well developed forechest. Brisket extends to elbow. *Ribs* long and well sprung but not barrel shaped, extending well towards hindquarters. *Loin* short, muscular, wide and deep, with very little tuck-up. Slab-sideness, narrow chest, lack of depth in brisket, excessive tuck-up to be faulted.

Tail well set on, thick and muscular at the base, following the natural line of the croup. Tail bones extend to, but not below, the point of hock. Carried with merry action, level or with some moderate upward curve; never curled over back nor between legs.

Forequarters — Muscular, well coordinated with hindquarters and capable of free movement. *Shoulder blades* long and well laid back with upper tips fairly close together at withers. *Upper arms* appear about the same length as the blades, setting the elbows back beneath the upper tip of the blades, close to the ribs without looseness. *Legs*, viewed from the front, straight with good bone, but not to the point of coarseness. *Pasterns* short and strong, sloping slightly with no suggestion of weakness. Dewclaws on forelegs may be removed, but are normally left on.

Feet medium size, round, compact, and well knuckled, with thick pads. Excess hair may be trimmed to show natural size and contour. Splayed or hare feet to be faulted.

Hindquarters — Broad and strongly muscled. Profile of croup slopes slightly; the pelvic bone slopes at a slightly greater angle (approximately 30 degrees from horizontal). In a natural stance, the femur joins the pelvis at approximately a 90-degree angle; *stifles* well bent; *hocks* well let down with short, strong *rear pasterns*. *Feet* as in front. *Legs* straight when viewed from rear. Cow-hocks, spread hocks, and sickle hocks to be faulted.

Coat — Dense and water-repellent with good undercoat. Outer coat firm and resilient, neither coarse nor silky, lying close to body; may be straight or wavy. Untrimmed natural ruff; moderate feathering on back of forelegs and on underbody; heavier feathering on front of neck, back of thighs and underside of tail. Coat on head, paws, and front of legs is short and even. Excessive length, open coats, and limp, soft coats are very undesirable. Feet may be trimmed and stray hairs neatened, but the natural appearance of coat or outline should not be altered by cutting or clipping.

Color — Rich, lustrous golden of various shades. Feathering may be lighter than rest of coat. With the exception of graying or whitening of face or body due to age, any white marking, other than a few white hairs on the chest, should be penalized according to its extent. Allowable light shadings are not to be confused with white markings. Predominant body color which is either extremely pale or extremely dark is undesirable. Some latitude should be given to the light puppy whose coloring shows promise of deepening with maturity. Any noticeable area of black or other off-color hair is a serious fault.

Gait — When trotting, gait is free, smooth, powerful and well coordinated, showing good reach. Viewed from any position, legs turn neither in nor out, nor do feet cross or interfere with each other. As speed increases, feet tend to converge toward center line of balance. It is recommended that dogs be shown on a loose lead to reflect true gait.

Temperament — Friendly, reliable, and trustworthy. Quarrelsomeness or hostility towards other dogs or people in normal situations, or an unwarranted show of timidity or nervousness, is not in keeping with Golden Retriever character. Such actions should be penalized according to their significance.

DISQUALIFICATIONS

Deviation in height of more than one inch from standard either way. Undershot or overshot bite.

Approved October 13, 1981
Reformatted August 18, 1990

Golden Oldies: A Bit of History

The written histories and origins of dog breeds come from kennel records, documents, letters, anecdotes, previously written breed histories, or stories passed down from one generation to another. Several modern breeds of obscure origin have been attributed to specific periods of ancient history because of similar-looking dogs depicted on stone carvings, artifacts, coins, or works of art from the period. Other breed histories may be part fact and part legend, the result of doubtful information combined with imaginative speculation. As in all facets of history, facts are elusive and difficult to prove. It is probably best to accept such breed chronicles as historical guideposts. However, they are all interesting to read and enjoyable to consider.

Happily, the account of the Golden Retriever's origin is very specific and well documented. The Golden Retriever was developed as a separate and distinctive dog breed in Scotland, beginning in the mid-1860s. The breed's origin can be authenticated by the kennel records kept from 1835 to 1890 by the gamekeepers at the estate of Sir Dudley Marjoribanks, the first Lord Tweedmouth, at Inverness, Scotland. The *stud book* entries record the essential information of planned matings, including dates, breeds, names of the dogs and the bitches, the resulting puppies' names and sex, and other important facts. From this one can trace the line of dogs that evolved into the Golden Retriever. The kennel records of Lord Tweedmouth are a priceless model of canine genealogy and early pedigree formulation. They are preserved and available for viewing at the Kennel Club in London, and are prized for their historical significance.

It was only as recently as 1952 that these records were made available to a writer-researcher by Lord Tweedmouth's great-nephew, the sixth Earl of Ilchester. *Country Life,* an English magazine, published the account of how the breed was created and stabilized, closing the book on a colorful but inaccurate story about the origin of the breed.

Prior to the release of Lord Tweedmouth's records, it was believed that the Golden Retriever was the result of his fascination with a troupe of unusual performing dogs in a traveling show, around 1860. The legend contended that the canine performers were from a strain of Russian circus dogs; that Lord Tweedmouth purchased them; that he used them to develop the Golden Retriever. The story had been widely circulated and accepted as fact for almost one hundred years when it was finally proved to be completely inaccurate by Tweedmouth's published kennel records.

Throughout the nineteenth century, hunting birds for sport and food was an important activity in the British Isles, especially in England and Scotland. Game was plentiful during that period, and a gun dog that could hunt and retrieve water fowl as well as upland birds was highly desirable. This encouraged the development and popularity of all the dogs that became the Retriever breeds.

The development of the *Golden* Retriever was set in motion in the mid-1860s with a purchase by Lord Tweedmouth of an unusual yellow puppy, which stood out in a litter of Wavy-Coated Black Retrievers, similar to the Flat-Coated Retriever of today. The uncommon yellow puppy, named Nous, was taken to Tweedmouth's kennels in Scotland to become the foundation dog for a new line of yellow Retrievers. At maturity, Nous was mated with Belle, one of several Tweed Water Spaniels kept at Lord Tweedmouth's kennels.

The Tweed Water Spaniel, now extinct, is described as a hardy Spaniel that was used for retrieving game in a variety of outdoor conditions. The coat of the Tweed Water Spaniel was close-curled, slightly feathered, and liver- or sandy-colored.

A litter of four puppies were born from the mating of Nous and Belle: Crocus, Primrose, Cowslip, and Ada. For the next twenty years, Lord Tweedmouth developed his much-admired line of "Yellow Retrievers" out of this first litter. The result was the creation of a new breed that ultimately became the Golden Retriever.

Lord Tweedmouth's breeding program included crosses with several Tweed Water Spaniels, an Irish Setter, a Wavy-Coated Black Retriever, and possibly a Bloodhound.

The importance of the Tweed Water Spaniel in the development of the modern Golden Retriever should not be minimized, even though the breed has long since disappeared. Its genetic influence continues. For many years this breed hunted along the shores of the Tweed River near Inverness by the side of Scottish hunters. It was descended from robust water dogs that lived with families along the rough British seacoast. They were fearless, dependable dogs that could retrieve downed birds no matter where they fell.

By the turn of the century, the popularity of the Yellow or Golden Retriever began an ascendancy that has never diminished. The breed won its first field trial in 1904 and was first shown in England at the Crystal Palace show of 1908. These Yellow Retrievers were listed as "Flat Coats (Golden)." The breed continued to be shown in England but was grouped with other Retrievers and listed as "Flat Coats." It was not until 1913 that they were accepted as a separate breed by the Kennel Club (England) and shown as Golden or Yellow Retrievers. With the formation of the Golden Retriever Club (of England) it was inevitable that they would make their appearance in the United States and take root in the imagination of American dog lovers.

The first Goldens came to American and Canadian shores as tourists, accompanied by their human companions, during the 1890s. Throughout the 1920s and the 1930s Golden Retrievers came to stay and became established throughout the Pacific and Atlantic states.

The first registration of a Golden Retriever by the American Kennel Club was in November 1925. While there had been Goldens registered before that date, they had been registered as Retrievers with some description as to color. In Canada, their first registration as a separate breed was in 1927.

The Golden Retriever Club of America was formed in 1938. For

Goldens have always been admired for their abilities as gun dogs and continue to be popular with bird hunters.

the first few decades, Goldens in America were admired for their magnificent abilities as gun dogs and were mostly owned by bird hunters. Many of the early American breeders held the line and bred for Goldens that were born to work in the field despite their good looks. However, the American Dog Fancy would not be denied and made early efforts to enter them in conformation shows. Inevitably, more and more of these breeders began exhibiting in the show ring.

English and Scottish field trials would run Goldens with both dark and light coats. The same was true in the British show ring. However, dogs of dark- to medium-gold coats were favored by breeders, exhibitors, and show judges. Despite the broad spectrum of coat color to choose from, the most experienced Golden fancier looks for balance, soundness, gait, trainability, and temperament. These qualities are far more important than coat color.

In 1936 the light-colored coat was incorporated into the English breed standard, making it as acceptable as the darker colors. Eventually, the lighter-colored Goldens entered the United States as English and Scottish imports but dogs with both light and dark coats continued to be brought over to satisfy the growing demand for this breed. A bias toward the darker-coated dogs continues to exist, although a light dog does occasionally win in the show ring because of other exceptional qualities.

It is important to note that the first three dogs of any breed to earn the AKC Obedience Champion title, in July 1977, were Golden Retrievers.

The breed's physical beauty and its sweet nature play a large role in its popularity in North America. Goldens' desire to please almost makes one forget their brilliance in the field.

With all of the breeds available for those desiring a pet, the Golden Retriever has consistently been among the most sought after dogs in America, year after year after year. Although approximately 65,000 individual Goldens are registered each year with the American Kennel Club, twice that many are born to AKC-registered litters annually. Half the AKC Golden Retrievers born annually are never even registered as individual dogs. Add to these annual figures the thousands that are registered with the United Kennel Club, and the number of Golden puppies moving into American homes becomes enormous. What it means is that the Golden Retriever, which has been in existence little more than a century, has become one of the most successful dog breeds in modern canine history.

CHAPTER THREE

Amazing Golden Retrievers

The Golden Retriever is a star. It is a breed that is popular with everyone who loves dogs, from pet owners to veterinarians to breeders, handlers, dog trainers, and even with people who do not live with one. Goldens are frequently seen in movies and on television because of their endearing and entertaining qualities. Many TV commercials feature a Golden Retriever because of the breed's good looks, sweet nature, and warm-hearted personality. They are effective salesdogs. But that is only part of the reason for their enormous popularity.

Few breeds are as versatile as Golden Retrievers. They are blessed with a keen intelligence combined with a touching desire to please those with whom they live. Since their first appearance they have been admired and prized for their considerable hunting and retrieving skills. But there is much more to the Golden Retriever story. They have excelled beyond all expectations at conformation shows, field trials, hunting tests, obedience trials, and dog agility tournaments.

Goldens are especially respected and cherished for their extraordinary ability to assist physically challenged human beings. The breed has become an integral part of all assistance dog programs. They are among a handful of breeds that are used as Service Dogs (for those in wheelchairs), as Hearing Dogs (for deaf people), as Therapy Dogs, and as Guide Dogs for those who are blind. Goldens are highly desirable for this work because they are intelligent, dependable dogs that love to work and please.

The greatest achievement of the breed, however, is its enormous success as a companion animal and canine member of the family.

These Golden dogs have been permanently woven into the tapestry of human life as loving friends and devoted partners. Golden Retrievers are truly amazing.

Dog Shows

There are two types of sanctioned dog shows, *Specialty* shows and *All-Breed* shows. Specialty shows are open to one specific breed of dog only or to a group of specific breeds. All-Breed shows are open to any breed, so long as it is recognized by the governing body, such as the American Kennel Club or the United Kennel Club, and so long as there are a sufficient number of entries to afford competition.

A dog show, which is more formally known as a conformation show, is a sports event in which dogs compete to win points in order to earn an AKC or UKC Champion title (Ch.). Once the title is earned, it will appear before the dog's name in all AKC or UKC records as well as in any written reference to the dog. Becoming a champion of record is a major achievement for a dog and its owner and is not easily accomplished.

According to the American Kennel Club:

To become an official American Kennel Club champion of record, a dog must earn fifteen points. A dog can earn from one to five points at a show. Wins of three, four, or five points are termed "majors." The fifteen points required for championship must be won under at least three different judges, and must include two "majors" won under different judges.

The United Kennel Club requires the following:

U.K.C. SHOW CHAMPION (CH.) — Qualifications for a U.K.C. Champion: (1) must have a minimum of one hundred (100) U.K.C. points; (2) must have shown and acquired Championship points under at least three different U.K.C. licensed judges; (3) must have won two Best Males/Females under two different U.K.C. licensed judges.

U.K.C. GRAND SHOW CHAMPION (GR. CH.) — Earned by winning: five (5) Champion of Champions show classes; in at least five (5) different U.K.C. licensed conformation shows; under at least three (3) different U.K.C. licensed judges.

Dog shows, or conformation shows, attract the largest number of participants in the dog sport and receive the greatest attention from the media and the general public. Conformation shows are seen on television and written about extensively in books, articles, and news stories. Among the most important AKC conformation shows in the United States are the Westminster Kennel Club Show (New York), the International Kennel Club Show (Chicago), the Santa Barbara Kennel Club Show (California), and such combined or "cluster" shows as the River City Cluster in San Antonio, and many, many others. The most important UKC event is the United Kennel Club Premier (Kalamazoo, Michigan) involving two All-Breed conformations shows, obedience trials, agility tournaments, Specialty shows, group shows, and other competitions and demonstrations.

Goldens at the Westminster Kennel Club Show in New York.

The show judge must consider many aspects of the dog besides its good looks.

Conformation shows are disparaged by some as being merely beauty pageants for dogs. One may argue that there is nothing wrong with beauty pageants. Dog shows, however, are more than that. Although each dog's physical attractiveness is part of the competition at a conformation show, structure, movement, temperament, and personality are also evaluated and given equal if not greater importance by the show judges.

The original purpose of the conformation show was to identify those dogs that possessed a body structure most suitable for the breed's function and to select them for mating. The idea was, and still is, to improve the breed. To many spectators at a dog show, all the dogs in the ring appear to be beautiful as well as animated, and they find it difficult to guess which one is the winner. The show judge, however, considers many aspects of the dogs. His or her responsibility is to examine each dog thoroughly, compare it to the written breed standard, and determine how close it comes to the ideal, to being the *perfect* Golden Retriever. The dog that comes closest to the breed standard wins. There is considerable competition at a dog show and a great deal of excitement for those involved. That is why it is called the dog sport. The competition is intense.

Golden Retrievers were entered in their first dog show in 1908 and again in 1909, at England's legendary Crystal Palace show, where they were listed as "Flat Coats (Golden)." By 1913 the Kennel Club (England) gave the breed separate status by color and allowed them to be listed as Golden or Yellow Retrievers.

Although the breed was first seen in the United States and Canada around 1890, it was not until 1925 that the first dog was registered with the American Kennel Club as a Golden Retriever rather than as a Retriever with a color designation. The first Golden was registered in Canada as a separate breed in 1927. In 1933 the first Golden in the United States became an American Kennel Club champion of record. It is important to understand that until that time Goldens were prized for their hunting abilities rather than for their dog show potential.

Over the decades the Golden has proven to be a consistent attraction in the show ring, setting high entry records in Golden Retriever Specialty shows as well as becoming a strong contender in All-Breed shows. This is reflected by the breed's enormous AKC and UKC registration numbers.

Once largely an owner-handled breed, the Golden is now strongly campaigned by professional handlers because of its greater quality of type, popularity with the audience, and its great appeal to the general public.

Anyone wishing to compete in conformation shows with a Golden Retriever should study the breed standard (see *Official Standard for the Golden Retriever* in Chapter 1, "Meet the Golden Retriever"), obtain the American Kennel Club or United Kennel Club's rules and regulations for dog shows, and seek the help and advice of a breeder or an exhibitor.

Obedience Trials

An obedience trial is a sporting event in which dogs and their handlers compete for winning points that accumulate toward an obedience title. The competition takes place before a crowd of spectators and consists of specific obedience exercises in accordance with American Kennel Club or United Kennel Club rules and regulations. As the name of the sport implies, dogs and their handlers must demonstrate their ability to perform established obedience routines to a high standard and are judged by licensed AKC or UKC judges, depending on the show.

The level of difficulty of the obedience exercises is determined by the categories of competition the dog enters. The *Novice Class* tests simple, practical obedience commands used in daily living, such as Heel on Leash, Heel Free, Long Sit, Long Down, etcetera. The Novice Class offers the AKC title of *Companion Dog* (C.D.), proudly shown after the dog's name. The UKC Novice Class title is U-CD.

The *Open Class* consists of more demanding obedience exercises, such as Drop on Recall, Retrieve over High Jump, Broad Jump, etcetera. Dogs entering Open Class competition must have earned a C.D. title from the Novice Class. The Open Class enables a dog to earn the title *Companion Dog Excellent* (C.D.X.). The UKC Open Class title is U-CDX.

The *Utility Class* offers dogs a high level of challenge in obedience trials for both dog and handler. It is a very demanding class, requiring near perfection in all exercises, some of which are Signal Exercise, Scent Discrimination, Directed Jumping, etcetera. Dogs competing in the Utility Class can earn the title *Utility Dog* (U.D.). Since January 1994, dogs in AKC obedience trials can earn a new title, *Utility Dog Excellent* (U.D.X.). Dogs with a U.D. or U.D.X. are eligible to compete for championship points for the highest possible title, *Obedience Trial Champion* (OTCh.). The UKC class title is U-CDX.

In 1947 the first Golden Retriever, Goldwood Toby, a male, earned the Utility Dog title (U.D.). Since then the breed has been a force to reckon with in the obedience ring. The first dog *ever* to win a U.D.X. was Casanova Rover, a Golden Retriever, in March 1994.

In 1977 the American Kennel Club introduced its prestigious national event the *Obedience Trial Championship*, offering the most important prize attainable for an obedience dog-handler team, *Obedience Trial Champion* (OTCh.). It is the only AKC obedience title placed *before* the dog's name.

The first dog of any breed to win the title Obedience Trial Champion was a female Golden, OTCh. Moreland's Golden Tonka. The first conformation champion to win an obedience trial championship was also a Golden, Ch. Russo's Gold Rush Sensation, a female. No other breed in obedience competition events has matched the prominence of the Golden Retriever, whose trainability and desire to please has made obedience competition its most outstanding sport involvement.

Tracking Tests

Tracking tests entail being outdoors in rugged terrain, hiking through mud and leaves, and trailing behind a Golden Retriever as he uses his natural scenting ability, an activity for the energetic dog owner. Following man-made tracks aged by time with turns of increasing difficulty and distance is an exercise in which your Golden is the leader and you are the follower. The tests are strictly pass-or-fail events under strict American Kennel Club guidelines for judging, and Goldens have excelled in them.

Tracking tests are also conducted by the United Kennel Club. Successfully completed tracking tests offer the titles *Tracking Dog* (TD) and *Tracking Dog Excellent* (TDX) to be applied following the dog's registered name in written references to him. Tracking requires a great deal of training for both dog and owner as a dog-handler team for the actual test. The tracking titles are not easily attained and only a few dogs have earned them. The scents are laid one half hour before the test for the TD title and no less than three hours before the start for the TDX title. The officials allow one personal item (such as

Getting the scent at a tracking test.

a glove) at the starting place and three other personal items along the trail and at varied intervals.

A dog being tested is harnessed to a twenty- to forty-foot leash held by the handler. The handler must remain at least twenty feet behind the dog. All dogs entered in the AKC tracking tests must go through a screening process that certifies them for the main event. Observing a tracking test is recommended before you attempt to become involved.

Agility Trials

An agility trial is a tournament in which individual dogs run through an obstacle course that tests their endurance, speed, and accuracy as their handlers direct them along the way. Each course must be run within a set time, which adds to the tension and excitement. With the crowd cheering the dogs on over A-frames and walls, through tunnels and weave poles, and up and down teetering see-saws, this is probably the most rousing of all the dog sports and the most fun for spectators. All dogs entering an agility trial must have speed and intelligence and have had precision training.

The agility trial was devised in England specifically for the 1978 Crufts Dog Show. It was envisioned as a minor diversion to amuse the spectators during a lull between various segments of the dog show. The event turned into a huge crowd pleaser and made a lasting impression. The pace of the demonstration was much faster than that of obedience trials and conformation judging. The enthusiasm and skill of the dogs was exciting to the audience, which responded with applause, whistles, and screams of approval as have audiences continued to do at agility events since the beginning.

This newest of sports for dog-and-owner competition was sure to emerge in the United States along with the popularity of fly-ball, scent hurdles, relay races, and other demonstration sports that have captured the imagination and attention of dog owners and dog lovers alike.

The sport of agility began to grow in popularity in this country after it became organized in 1986 by the United States Dog Agility Association (USDAA). This organization set standards, adopted rules, and created certified titles to be awarded for achievement in various levels of competition. There are three classes of competition: *Novice*, *Open*, and *Excellent*. With each class the required speed increases along with the number and complexity of the obstacles. Jumps are adjusted to the size of the dogs.

Enhancing the future of agility trials in the United States is the American Kennel Club's acceptance of the sport as part of its roster of sanctioned dog events. The AKC's first licensed agility trial took place on August 11, 1995, in Houston, at the Astro World Series of Dog Shows. The event was a huge success, with 192 entries represented by 58 breeds. Of all the entries only four dogs were first-place winners in the Excellent class. Among them was Miss Molly's Paradise, a Golden Retriever.

In agility trials, dogs run through an obstacle course that tests their endurance, speed, and accuracy.

Search and Rescue (SAR) Dogs

Goldens have entered the field of search and rescue in an important way and have been successful at finding lost people and disaster victims. With their strong sense of smell, desire to please, and love of people, they are a natural breed for this heroic activity.

The dogs must be trained in tracking, obedience, and agility-type courses to be prepared for the terrain they encounter as they search for plane crash, earthquake, and disaster victims. They must be well socialized from puppyhood on, as they will have to travel extensively with humans and other dogs to search-and-rescue sites. Dog-handler teams must be in excellent physical condition in order to work long, hard hours in rugged terrain and in extreme temperatures and weather conditions.

When a rescue mission is successful, the dog's joy at the *find*, or moment of discovery, is very great. However, in natural-disaster situations, Goldens often become depressed at the find if the victims are already dead. This unusually sad and touching behavior gives the impression that the dogs equate finding a dead victim with failure. To offset depression at a disaster site when the work must continue, live victims are occasionally "arranged" to restore the dog's spirit.

Search-and-rescue teams must be certified by the National Association of Search and Rescue (NASAR), located in Fairfax, Virginia, and are on call 24 hours a day, 365 days a year. In spite of the hard training, difficult working conditions, and tragedy encountered, no greater joy is shared than between the Golden, his handler, and the victim who is saved from disaster by the search-and-rescue team.

Field Trials and Working Certificate Tests

The Golden's original purpose was to assist the hunter to retrieve upland game and water fowl. To this day Goldens are still the companions and partners of many hunters. All of the hunting breeds were working dogs whose place in the family depended on their assistance

in putting food on the table. An owner couldn't afford to feed or house a dog that didn't earn his keep. The greater the ability of the dog, the better he was treated and the more he was held in esteem.

It was natural for hunters to brag about the abilities of their dogs—which one was faster, which had the best nose, and so on. This friendly rivalry was quite likely the basis for establishing the first field trial competitions. Today field trials are extremely high-tech competitions, with point schedules, titles, and ratings. Competing in such trials as well as traveling to the events is very expensive. Competition begins with the selection of the dogs from proper bloodlines and demands rigorous training, which begins the moment the puppy is brought home.

A trial dog may compete for a Field Champion or Amateur Field Champion title. Separate field trials are held for specific breeds and groups of breeds. Rules and procedures vary for pointing breeds, Spaniels, Beagles, Basset Hounds, Dachshunds, and the retrieving breeds. Although Labrador Retrievers hold the number one position in entries, Goldens continue to hold their own, especially in the amateur stakes, which stress the bond and teamwork between the dog and his owner.

If you live in the city and do not like to hunt but would like to test your Golden's natural ability, the Working Certificate, or Hunting Test may be for you. The Working Certificate or WC Test was created by the Golden Retriever Club of America to keep the retriever ability in the breed.

Simple marking and retriever tests on land and water, with pass-fail scores, make it easy for the average Golden owner to test his or her dog's natural instincts with limited training and resources and no pressure of competition.

The American Kennel Club has recently created noncompetitive Hunting title tests, which are more difficult, have several levels, and stress actual hunting situations. The United Kennel Club also offers hundreds of Hunting Retriever tests all across the nation.

Therapy Dogs

Many Golden Retrievers are informally referred to as *Therapy Dogs* because their owners regularly take them to visit patients in hospitals, nursing homes, and other medical facilities where they give their love and affection to everyone. Most health-care providers believe in the medical benefits of bringing together emotionally hurting humans with dogs, whose boundless affection and unconditional acceptance are capable of breaching many emotional and psychological barriers.

Golden Retrievers enjoy this activity and benefit from it, too, because it gives them an opportunity to express their highly social behavior and love of people. When Goldens come to visit, they brighten the lives of patients in hospitals, nursing homes, old-age homes, as well as the disabled, psychiatric patients, abused children, and those in prison rehabilitation programs. Therapy Dogs perform their magic by making direct emotional contact with everyone and anyone, with no strings attached.

Since 1977 the Delta Society has fostered the concept of nurturing contact between humans and animals. The society is the leading international information clearinghouse and action center for the interaction of people, animals, and the environment and for animal-assisted therapy. This organization's studies on the effects of animals on human health have been the inspiration for Golden Retriever owners' generous therapy visits.

The Golden Retriever's even temperament and gentle, loving personality has made it one of the most welcome breeds in hospitals across the country. Goldens are also likely to spend much time with disturbed or depressed adults and will relate equally to the outgoing and talkative, the severely depressed, and even the abusive patient. Their generous expression of affection for everyone always evokes a friendly, happy response.

Patients who never talk to anyone will suddenly talk to a Golden and his handler, will stroke the dog's coat, and will perhaps become nostalgic about dogs they have known and loved, which may lead to other personal discussions. Some patients never say a word to anyone but will allow a dog to lay his head on their lap and look up as they stare at each other. Such patients are often drawn out of their depression and talk to the medical staff later, the topic of conversation being the dog that came to call.

Hospitalized children with emotional problems can be the most difficult for visiting dogs. Many such children are aggressive or hyperactive or completely withdrawn. They can be very rough and must be prevented from being abusive to the dogs. Fortunately, Golden Retrievers have a high tolerance for such behavior, even if it involves pushing, pulling, and screeching. Encouraging such children to comb and brush the dogs or simply talk to them often elicits a calmed, gentle response, depending on their mood and the severity of their problems. Through it all, Goldens will smile, wag, and tolerate most unruly behavior from young patients. The children often find touching ways to say thank you to the dogs for being their friends, sometimes with a hug, sometimes with a handmade Christmas card.

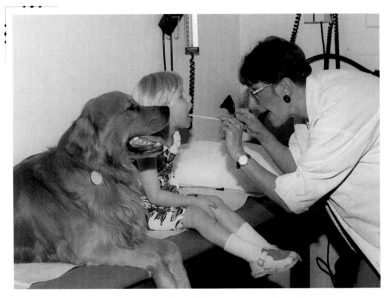

Say, Ahh. *Therapy Dogs give sympathy and support to worried patients.*

Service Dogs

A Service Dog is one that has been trained to work with people with physical disabilities. These remarkable dogs are always with their disabled partners and perform such important tasks as pulling wheelchairs, manipulating simple household appliances, turning lights on and off, opening cupboard doors, and retrieving out-of-reach or dropped items. These seemingly simple chores assume enormous importance to disabled persons. Dogs help them enjoy greater independence in most aspects of their lives. Service Dogs make it possible for their partners to go to school, get a job, travel, and in general enjoy a full life.

The concept of the Service Dog was created by Dr. Bonita M. Bergin, who as a young woman traveled abroad working as a teacher. The idea came to her while teaching in Australia and traveling throughout Asia and Europe, where she discovered that disabled people in other countries were more self-reliant and independent by necessity. She observed that many of them used donkeys and other manageable pack animals for assistance.

In the mid-1970s, Bergin returned to the United States and eventually developed the idea of training dogs to assist disabled people. By the early 1980s, after several years of struggle and sacrifice, she had structured a basic program for acquiring specific dogs, training them, and making them available to those willing to try them out. She incorporated and named her infant organization Canine Companions for Independence (CCI). This remarkable operation has grown over the years as a major force for good throughout the United States, with branches in a number of metropolitan areas. She established rapport with other assistance-dog organizations and founded Assistance Dogs International, an amalgam of similar training programs inviting membership from other countries.

Service Dogs are trained to assist those with physical disabilities, particularly those who use wheelchairs. Another category of assistance dogs provided by CCI is the Hearing Dog. Hearing Dogs are for people who are deaf and hard of hearing. They alert their human partners to crucial sounds such as doorbells, ringing telephones, alarm clocks, smoke alarms, crying children, and so on. Although Golden Retrievers can function as Hearing Dogs, only a few are selected for that service.

The greatest number of Service Dogs are Golden Retrievers. Other breeds utilized are Labrador Retrievers, Border Collies, and Pembroke Welsh Corgis.

Guide Dogs for People Who Are Blind

The Golden Retriever who guides his blind partner is described as kind of heart, friendly, intelligent, with no sign of fear or aggression, sensitive, and dedicated to duty. As one of the three breeds used by Guide Dog institutions, the Golden Retriever is chosen for its size, coat, temperament, and willingness to work. Puppies are raised in volunteer homes to socialize them and familiarize them with most sit-

Golden retrievers' size, temperament, and willingness to work make them ideal Guide Dogs.

uations. They are returned to their respective schools between the ages of twelve and eighteen months of age to begin rigorous training and testing. Only the best will be chosen for three to six months of additional training and extensive hard work and will then be matched with a blind partner. The dog-human team are then given on-premise training and situational work in busy traffic and on public transportation.

The pioneering Guide Dog school in the United States, the Seeing Eye, in Morristown, New Jersey, was established in 1929. It was inspired by earlier work with blinded veterans done in Germany after the First World War. Buddy, a German Shepherd Dog, and her blind partner, Morris Frank, a founder of the Seeing Eye, trained in Switzerland and came back to the United States, where Frank publicized the advantages of working with a Guide Dog. Currently there are fourteen active programs functioning in the United States and three in Canada.

The dogs are given to the blind partner at no charge. This is made possible by donations from many concerned people upon whom all existing schools and programs depend. The Golden has been so successful at giving newfound independence to its blind teammate that a New York couple, Ed and Toni Eames, now relocated in Fresno, California, have become the first blind obedience handlers to train their Goldens to American Kennel Club CD and CDX titles and Bermudan CDs. They write a feature column for *Dog World* magazine, the title of which clearly describes their relationship with their Goldens, "Partners in Independence."

The Eameses are the authors of the book *A Guide To Guide Dog Schools* and team-teach workshops and seminars dealing with disability issues for teachers, veterinarians, and others interested in the subject. Toni Eames has a master's degree in rehabilitation counseling from Hunter College. Ed Eames has a Ph.D. from Cornell University and is a retired professor of anthropology from Temple University and Baruch College.

The Eameses believe that the goal of giving independence to a blind person is achieved when a dog-human team have the freedom and ability to travel in comfort and safety. In their book they state, "Approximately 8,000 guide dog teams are presently working in Canada and the United States. Since there is an estimated population of 750,000 blind and visually impaired people in these countries, it means fewer than 1.5% of them use guide dogs as their basic means of mobility. One reason for this low percentage, we believe, is lack of information about these remarkable canine assistants. Our goal is to fill this information gap."

To order their book *A Guide to Guide Dog Schools* send $10 to: Ed and Toni Eames, 3376 N. Wishon, Fresno, CA 93704-4832. Make checks payable to Disabled on the Go (D.O.G.). See the Appendix for a listing of Guide Dog schools.

The Eameses tell us in their book that the three breeds most commonly used as Guide Dogs are Labrador Retrievers, Golden Retrievers and German Shepherd Dogs.

Drug and Arson Detection Dogs

Since 1970 the U.S. Customs Service has employed dogs for use in drug detection. The Golden Retriever is one of three breeds used for this work. With an eager personality, a desire to retrieve, and a good scenting nose, they are well suited for this work. Through extensive reward training the dogs are employed to sniff out narcotics at airports, maritime facilities, and post offices, resulting in thousands of drug seizures, with the street value running in the hundreds of millions of dollars.

Drug awareness cards issued by the U.S. Customs Service have pictures of Golden Retrievers on them with information regarding the dogs' age, weight, years in service, and a list of their largest and most notable seizures. The cards are distributed at schools for trading and collecting by children in order to promote and support the drug-free message.

Arson Dogs have been known to detect fire-causing agents in amounts so infinitesimal that not even forensic laboratories could identify them. These fire-sniffing dogs are given reward training similar to that of Drug Detection Dogs and are taught to signal their handlers when they find what they are after. With their highly developed scenting ability, Arson Dogs are trained to sniff out and signal that they have found materials with fire-causing accelerants no matter how obscurely located—under water, ice, or piles of debris. The Arson Dog's purpose is to help fire marshals figure out how or what started a fire. The dogs' findings reveal whether a fire was started deliberately and make an important contribution to finding the culprit. The preferred breeds for this work are the German Shepherd Dog and the Golden Retriever.

Dogs in Movies, TV, and Advertising

Turn on the TV, pick up a magazine, go to the movies, and sooner rather than later you'll be looking at a Golden. With their smiling faces, handsome color, and friendly attitude they are naturals for film and print. In any situation you can picture a family in, especially with kids, you'll see a Golden. Goldens can sell dog food, cars, homes, or just about anything on TV and are always a show business presence. The Walt Disney film *The Incredible Journey* was remade as *Homeward Bound* and used a Golden Retriever as its star instead of the original Labrador Retriever. From Brandon on *Punky Brewster* to Comet on *Full House*, Goldens are seen everywhere on television. Lindsay Wagner sells Ford automobiles with Goldens and personally gave out the Gaines Superdog top trophy to a Golden in the top obedience competition. Goldens sell warmth and trust and safety in their actors' role as your best friend. The truth is, it's no act.

Golden Retrievers are truly amazing.

CHAPTER FOUR

The Golden Bond

The Right Way to Love Your Puppy

Bonding is simply the creation of a strong emotional connection based on a growing relationship. When people do not bond with their dogs they find it harder to train them, harder to control them, harder to enjoy them, but, unfortunately, easier to part with them. When a Golden Retriever first comes into your home, bonding with him is the first thing you should accomplish, even before training. Bonding with your dog is the most important thing you can do.

Everyone loves a puppy. The first time he enters his home as a frisky, uninhibited youngster, his new family finds his energy, curiosity, and comical mischief exhilarating. Despite the little dog's howling through the first night or two and his confusion as to where to relieve himself, everyone enjoys playing with him. This interlude of good feeling, unfortunately, may not last. Puppies grow up, and many new dog owners, having never considered what their adorable canine babies might be like as adult dogs, are surprised by the great differences in size, looks, and behavior. Living with a dog requires accepting him in the various stages of his life. The delightful antics and cute looks of a puppy inevitably come to an end; change is the only constant factor.

Sustaining love for a pet throughout his lifetime requires the creation of an emotional bond that holds the dog and his family together in a happy, satisfying relationship. If the value of creating a bond is understood, a pet dog will always be loved and cared for, especially in old age.

Puppy characteristics are eventually replaced by the endearing qualities of grown dogs, such as their love and devotion for those they live with, their participation in everyday family life, and the attention and companionship they lavishly give. Adult Goldens are much more interesting than puppies. As grown-ups they are athletes that love to run, play, swim, retrieve, and do anything you want as long as it seems like fun. Full-grown Goldens are happiest when they are with you. They relate to their family members in the most meaningful way and stir the heart as few other living creatures can. They are among the most caring animals.

Like most dogs, Golden Retrievers have no difficulty bonding with all family members, and they do it in a matter of minutes. It is in their nature. Once the bond is established, it remains for a lifetime unless a dog is abused or neglected.

Not all dog owners, however, bond with their pets. Many are simply not aware of the concept, its importance, its benefits, or how to do it, despite the fact that bonding is as natural for people as it is for dogs.

How to Bond with Your Golden Retriever

Creating an emotional bond with a dog involves generous expressions of love and affection, talk, socializing, play, and training.

Love and affection as a bonding technique

Golden puppies are irresistible; if you come within six feet of one, you cannot escape the urge to hold it, hug it, and kiss it. The desire to express your feelings so openly is good for the pup, good for you, and good for both of you together. That desire is the essence of bonding. Long after puppyhood the shared feelings will remain through good times and bad times. Goldens have the ability to understand and sympathize with your every mood. It is this quality that brings them so close to their owners. Most people who live with a Golden have said at one time or another, "He understands how I feel. He knows what I'm thinking." But these are the comments of those who have bonded with their dogs.

Freely expressing your affection not only cultivates your dog's personality, it creates a strong, unbreakable bond and then keeps reinforcing it on a daily basis. A puppy left alone in the yard will still love its owner. Goldens are like that. Leaving the dog out of your activities, however, fails to establish the bond that makes him a member of the family and an important part of your life.

Golden Retrievers love people unconditionally, *just because they exist*. If you raise a pup with the idea that he is loved and wanted, he will always be at his best when you teach him something. He will always be a *"good dog."* Puppies are innocent. They do not chew the rug or pee on the floor on purpose. All they want is to eat, play, and be loved by the people in their lives who are their leaders.

If you never place your dog in a situation in which he fails or is bad, he will always consider himself a great dog living a happy life. This is a matter of owner attitude and behavior. A supportive, approving attitude encourages a puppy to grow into a dog with self-confidence, to love and trust you, to work with you, and to accept your leadership role in his life. Most important, it establishes and deepens the bond between you and your dog. Love and affection are the very essence of a bond between a dog and his family.

Talking to your dog as a bonding technique

Talk to your dog. If you do, your puppy or your adult dog will always run to you with enthusiasm at the sound of your voice. Never yell or allow your voice to show anger or hysteria. This is important even if you are reprimanding your pet. In dog training a voice correction requires a firm but *controlled* tone of voice in two- or three-word sentences. (See Corrections in Chapter 8, "Obedience-Training Your Golden Retriever.")

Goldens are extremely sensitive to your moods and postures and respond to them more than to any harsh reprimands you can bellow out. Sometimes direct eye contact and a stiff posture are all that is needed to indicate your displeasure with your dog's behavior.

While your dog is still a puppy, try talking to him in a high-pitched tone of voice because it sounds pleasant and is not threatening. Talk to him about everything while hugging him, kissing him, and touching him.

Touch is a major part of bonding. Touch him on his eyes, his nose, his feet, and his back. If you talk to your dog at the same time you touch him, the bonding deepens as it communicates your feelings for him. Your dog will always want to be with you. Talk to your puppy as you would talk to a child. Even though your dog won't understand exactly what you are saying, he will understand your feelings for him.

When you talk to your Golden Retriever, punctuate your conversations by accentuating key words in your speech along with happy-sounding variations in your tone of voice. Explain things and ask questions; this will strengthen the bond.

If your dog makes you angry, the most effective reprimand you can give is to ignore him. Goldens cannot stand that and immediately want to make up and please you. For the purpose of bonding, talk to your dog in a kind, gentle, affectionate way. And do it often.

Socializing as a bonding technique

Your new Golden Retriever should be exposed to as many new people, noises, places, and situations as possible, soon after his vaccinations are effective. Allow him to socialize with other people and other dogs, where practical. Take him everywhere in your car: on short trips to shops, to the car wash, on social visits with your friends, and so forth, where you can carry him in. Everybody wants to pet a puppy. Being petted will socialize your dog and get him accustomed to new people and places. This will have a profound influence on the developing bond between you. He will very much appreciate your taking him places. If you have more than one dog, this will be a special time for him to be with you exclusively. Socializing is an important aspect of bonding.

Everyone knows that a Golden Retriever is not a one-man dog. He will love everyone and everything without diminishing his feelings for you, his teacher and best friend. This is not a protection or guard breed, so it is normal for your dog to welcome everyone who comes to your home. Although the adult Golden will announce the presence of a stranger, serving as a deterrent against trouble, he is immediately thrilled when anyone enters and greets people like an old friend.

The flip side of socializing is teaching your puppy to stay alone. This should start the day he comes to live with you. Place him in his crate and allow him to lie quietly as you leave the room. It will not be a big deal if you do not make it one. Come and go matter-of-factly with no hugs or overly enthusiastic talk. Do not gush or make guilt-ridden promises. Do not build up your dog's expectations when you leave with statements about coming back *reeeaal soon!*

The same applies when you return. Do not make a big emotional production of it. This only serves to create anxiety and restlessness about being left alone. On your return do not tell the dog what a

A well-socialized Golden is at ease with new people and places.

good boy he was. Do not crate him immediately before leaving and do not release him the minute you return. Maintain a casual air. Simply open the crate door when it is convenient and go about your business. Playtime can come shortly afterward. However, if your puppy is on a housebreaking schedule, do not release him in the house until he has had an opportunity to relieve himself outside.

During the first week with your new dog, make several short, unscheduled trips to the store or around the block. Come and go at irregularly timed intervals alternately using the front and back doors. When you return, resume some household chore before releasing the puppy from his crate.

Socializing your dog properly and not creating separation anxiety develops the best possible bond between you and your pet.

Play as a bonding technique

Goldens are fun-loving dogs. They love to play, whether with you, other people, or other dogs. If there is no one to play with, they will amuse themselves with solitary games.

They love to walk, hike, swim, or do anything else you can do with them. Games of retrieval with a ball or toy are their greatest pleasure because bringing you things in their mouths is their most natural behavior. That is why they are called Retrievers. Retrieving a ball, of course, is good exercise and is the ultimate joy for Goldens. Nevertheless, some Golden Retrievers excel at other games.

Golden Retrievers vary in their personalities and degrees of intelligence. Do not expect all Goldens to excel in or even like the same games. Rather than just tossing your dog something to be retrieved, try a game that not only fulfills his need to play but stimulates his brain while increasing his vocabulary.

Try Where's the Baby. This game is best when your dog wants attention and you are busy with something else or are watching TV. It involves the new generation of chewable stuffed dog toys. Try the plush, furry toss toys that are soft and washable. The entire toy consists of nothing but an animal's head and face.

Every time you buy your dog a new stuffed animal, give it a name. The name could be a color or animal type. Keep it simple; for example, Brown Bear, Red Mouse, Blue Panda. Use two-syllable names. Look at your dog and ask for one of the toys by name. "Goldie, get Brown Bear."

Expect your dog to bring you anything he can grab in the beginning. Be patient. If the wrong toy is brought to you, ignore it and say, "No, Red Bear." After fifteen to twenty failures, eventually he will retrieve the right toy, by luck, of course. When he brings it, praise him lavishly and end the game. After five days of repetition with this toy switch to another.

Some dogs become quite adept at this game and learn to identify many of the toys by their names. Other dogs may never learn to identify more than one or two of the toys by name but will be enthusiastic about the game anyway. On the other hand, your dog may develop other skills, such as balancing toys on his muzzle.

Teaching your dog Where's the Baby may result in his learning to find lost objects for you when asked. Most Goldens will keep searching until they find what they're looking for. The downside is losing something important, such as your keys, and searching frantically only to find them in the dog's toy box, where they've been discarded in favor of Green Frog.

A word of caution regarding play. Remember not to laugh or encourage any play behavior in a puppy that is unacceptable for an adult dog, especially a Golden. Do not, for example, play tug-of-war. Games such as this promote aggressive behavior.

Bear in mind that Goldens have been bred to release their prize to the owner or hunter, not to chew on it or tear it. When working in the field, as they were bred to do, shaking a retrieved bird is undesirable. Tugging games involving an object held in the mouth pull against a puppy's teeth and improperly change the alignment. Always insist that any object brought to you must be released quickly. Lavishly praise your dog for doing this. Do not allow your Golden to resist opening his mouth and releasing whatever is in it. The one area where this doesn't apply is the dog's food.

If you don't have a swimming pool or lake to take your dog to, then buy a child's wading pool for your puppy or adult Golden. This is a must. A wading pool will provide many hours daily of cool, harmless fun for a young dog. It also offers a refreshing place to recline in hot weather. A hard-plastic wading pool (noninflatable) is inexpensive and can be thrown away at the end of the season. If it lasts the summer you must take it up and store it someplace, or your Golden will stand in it and dig with his front paws, trying to make the water come back.

Another way to play with your dog is to get involved with the various dog sports available for you and your Golden. These offer an opportunity to learn how to train your dog while competing with others.

There are conformation dog shows, obedience trials, tracking tests, the sport of agility (competitive obstacle courses), and fly-ball (relay races with a caught ball), which are all activities that Golden Retrievers have excelled in. Do not lose sight of the reason for the involvement: to have fun with your dog and help develop the bond. With that in mind the competition will always be play activity, and

you are always the winner because you have each other. You can't lose that way.

Training as a bonding technique

Dog training is essential for creating an adaptive pet that must survive in a human environment. However, an important side benefit is bonding.

When you obedience-train your dog, you develop the ability to control him. The process for doing this involves close, personal contact and direct communication between you and the dog. These are the essential ingredients for creating the emotional bond that is so necessary for a lasting relationship.

When training your dog in the proper way, which is to say using the motivational techniques of rewards and corrections, you must communicate on a meaningful level. You are required to convey to the dog your approval when he does the right thing and your disapproval when he does the wrong thing.

When you train your dog, you teach him to obey various commands that he must perform in a precise manner. The teaching process involves talking, touching, socializing, and, in a sense, playing. Whenever the dog does the right thing, he is lavishly praised and given a great deal of encouragement. When he does not obey, he is given a correction that may be a tug of the leash or a firm verbal reprimand. Both aspects of training involve communication; that is how bonding is accomplished. Even when housebreaking your dog, you are instructed to make a big fuss over him when he relieves himself in the right place. He must be walked and given his food and water on a frequent schedule. He must be confined to one area. He must be corrected for mistakes. These are all close-contact activities that create an involvement between the dog and his family. These, too, set the bond.

Other ways of bonding with your dog

Whatever mischief your puppy gets into that makes you laugh, such as going into the bathroom and stealing toilet paper, can be turned around as part of the bonding process.

You can bond with your dog by talking to him as you feed him. "Hey, here comes dinner. Here's chow, puppy." The puppy will gaze at you as you communicate.

You can bond with your dog when you're medicating him with eye drops or ear drops by trying to make it fun or by soothing his anxiety. You can bond when you groom him. Every time you touch him, you can talk to him and make it a happy occasion. Massaging your dog will create a feeling of relaxation for both of you as well as a feeling of physical communication.

Puppies have the same needs as babies. They need love, food, and nurturing. You cannot love them too much. You cannot be too good to them. To bond with your dog is to learn how to love him. Dogs that are bonded with their families usually have a strong desire to please them.

A new dog, young or old, must feel that he belongs, that he is a part of the family. Once this is accomplished, his desire to become part of the family is strong and the bond between you is in place.

CHAPTER FIVE

Golden Gear
What Your Dog Needs

To make the newest member of your family content and secure, you'll need some Golden gear. Shortly after your new dog scurries through the door and sniffs around the house for the first time, he is going to look for something to drink, something to eat, and a place to pee. Then he will introduce himself to everybody, explore his new domain, and expend his energy and joy on the family. After all that, you can be sure he will look for a cozy place to curl up in and take a nap, a place he can call his own.

In the beginning, your goal should be to gently convince your dog that this is now his home, that he is safe and sound, and that everything is just fine. To accomplish this will require proper handling, patience and understanding, and some dog equipment and supplies. Although a puppy's material needs are not extensive, they are important. If you want to start him off on the right paw, you should have on hand the Golden gear recommended here *before the dog arrives*.

A Wire Dog Crate

A wire crate (or *dog crate*) is a collapsible cage, made of thick metal wire with a solid metal floor (coated pan) and a hinged door at the front. Some crates also open from the top as an added safety feature, while others come with a slanted front, making them easier to fit into the back of a station wagon. A wire crate is an important investment for a new dog owner because it can be used in a number of valuable ways for the life of the dog. It is useful for confinement when house-

A wire crate can be used in a number of valuable ways throughout the life of a dog.

breaking and solving behavior problems and for preventing a dog from getting into trouble when he cannot be supervised. The crate also functions as an indoor doghouse, a place of his own, allowing the dog free access when the wire door is kept open. Once the crate is no longer needed to confine the dog it becomes a sanctuary, a safety area, a place to rest and get away from it all. The wire crate becomes the core area of your dog's territory almost immediately after it is introduced to him.

If you are going to drive your new dog home in the family car, it is advisable to get a wire crate beforehand so that you can transport your dog in safety and comfort. Although it is tempting to hold the puppy in your lap (as someone else drives), placing him in a wire crate is safer. A puppy's bones are soft and easily broken or dislocated if he flies out of your lap during a sudden stop or collision. The dog is less likely to be injured if he is in his crate. Spread a large towel on the bottom of the crate for traction, place the dog inside, close the wire door, and drive away. In the event the puppy has his own "accident," it will be easier to clean up the crate than the seat of the car. Leaving his previous home and adjusting to his first car ride is likely to upset his stomach, causing him to throw up or go to the toilet. Take a roll of paper towels and a large plastic bag with you.

Wire crates can be bought at many pet supply stores and in all pet supply catalogs. When selecting a crate, consider the current size of your Golden Retriever puppy and the full size he will grow to be. The crate you buy should allow your dog to sit up without hitting his head on the top and to lie down, stretched out completely. Start out with a crate that is slightly smaller than what he will need as an adult dog. Once the dog is fully grown, get one that is big enough for an adult Golden Retriever. It is more comforting for the dog if the inside is cozy and provides just a bit more room than his body needs. If there is too much interior space, the crate loses its den-like quality. An alternative to buying two different-size crates is to get one that is adult size and reduce the unneeded space by placing a wire crate divider inside (fixed to the sides of the crate) where needed, like a temporary wall. Such dividers can be purchased. Leave just enough room for the dog to lie down or sit up. As the weeks and months pass, keep moving the partition back as needed until the puppy grows into a full-size dog (approximately one year).

High-pile imitation lambskin pads spread across the bottom pan make the crate soft and cozy, making it very appealing to the dog. Considering the comfort offered by a crate, it is not unusual for a dog to go to his crate on his own. If you own more than one dog, they may both curl up together. A good wire crate (along with an exercise pen and a puppy gate) is a good investment in your dog's health and happiness. Therefore, it is recommended that you buy one of high quality that will last for years. A good crate should collapse for traveling ease and provide comfort for your dog. Newer epoxy crates offer beautiful designer colors to blend in with home decor. Remember, a sturdy dog crate helps to avoid chewed carpets and furniture and gives the dog owner peace of mind. A wire crate is a wise, considerate, humane piece of equipment when used properly and is extremely effective and useful. Other important uses for the crate and how to employ it can be found in chapters on housebreaking, paper training, obedience training, behavior problems, and bonding.

Super Bowls

Buying food and water bowls for your dog is not a simple matter. Catalogs and pet supply shops, especially the huge pet supply stores found in shopping malls, offer an incredible array of types, sizes, shapes, and materials. There may be more bowls to choose from than types of food to put in them. It helps to understand, however, that various bowl types function in different and useful ways.

Shape

The first consideration should be the shape of the bowl. Some bowls are wide at the bottom and narrow at the top and usually deeper than the average bowl. They are meant to be used by dogs with long, hanging ears. Bowls of this shape prevent the ears from sloshing in the bowl while allowing the dog to get at the food or water. Adult Golden Retrievers have ears of medium length and do not require this type of bowl, although it can be used. Also available are puppy pans that feature a raised center, leaving a circular channel around the outside, allowing more than one puppy to feed at the same time. Goldens should have their food and water given to them in conventional bowls with straight or slightly slanted sides and flat bottoms. If the dog is going to be fed on a smooth or slippery surface, such as linoleum, get a bowl with a rubber ring on the bottom to prevent it from sliding back and forth. Some bowls are heavily weighted on the bottom to discourage the dog from tipping them over.

Size

The average adult Golden Retriever needs a two-quart bowl; larger dogs require a three-quart bowl. The capacity of the bowl depends on the size of your dog, his appetite, and whether you live with more than one dog.

Twin elevated feeders are bowls that sit together in a sturdy metal rack so that they never touch the floor. These bowls can be obtained in various sizes and heights. They make it easier for a fully grown dog to eat, although you can achieve the same effect by placing conventional bowls on a stack of cinder blocks or on a milk carton. Elevated feeders prevent dogs from eating off the ground and avoid a lot of bending for dogs and pet owners. Raising your dog's food bowl can help to prevent the life-threatening condition known as *bloat* according to some. Many Golden Retriever show people believe food and water bowls should not be placed lower than their dogs' shoulders in order to develop and maintain good posture and a dignified presence.

Shallow bowls are made for smaller dogs (they hold less food) and deeper bowls are for larger dogs (they hold more food). Large, plastic, self-feeding bins are available which store large quantities of dry food and dispense a little at a time. Every time the dog eats, more food drops into the bottom tray. These bowls enable dogs to eat whenever they are hungry. You can also buy large and small motorized food containers that work with a timer, serving a measured amount of food at designated times.

Bowl materials

Most dog breeders agree that the best food and water bowls are made of stainless steel or stoneware. If you purchase a ceramic bowl, avoid those that were fired in the manufacturing process with a lead-base glaze, as they can lead to medical problems. Do not buy thin-gauge metal or plastic bowls, which can be chewed through quite easily, creating injuries if pieces are swallowed or scraping the inside of the mouth of a persistent puppy or a bored dog. Thick, hard plastic bowls of high quality are acceptable though not as durable as stainless steel. Some breeders believe that plastic bowls can actually change the color of a dog's nose. Golden Retriever breeders use large stainless-steel buckets for water or for carrying large quantities of dog food. These are practical, efficient, and hygienic.

Dog Beds

All puppies should have a cozy bed to sleep on. When a puppy leaves its mother and litter mates, you can help it get over the bewildering

Every dog appreciates a soft, comfortable bed.

change in its life with a warm, soft bed, which will serve as a substitute for the comfort of the nest.

Although nothing can truly replace the beat of his mother's heart or the reassurance of her breathing, a soft dog bed helps your puppy a great deal. If he came from a source other than a kennel, where he curled up with other dogs, he has slept on shredded paper or cedar chips with or without other puppies not related to him, and a bed of his own will be an appreciated change. Either way, a comfortable dog bed will help the newest member of your family make an easier adjustment to his home.

A blanket or a large towel placed in a corner of the room is adequate. These can be washed easily and if they are chewed up will not create a hardship for anyone. For a more pleasing appearance pillow-like, basket-type, and doghouse-type dog beds are sold in pet supply stores and mail-order catalogs. They come in a wide variety of prices, types, and levels of luxury. All of them are satisfactory. You will never hear a word of complaint from your dog.

In addition to dog beds, you can also find manufactured dog blankets designed to resist the digging, chewing, and soiling behavior of puppies; acrylic fake-fur pet beds in various sizes and shapes; dog pillows with washable covers; padded or inflatable floor mats that are lightweight and easy to pack in a suitcase; orthopedic dog beds and travel beds that fit into the backseat of a car and attach to the seat belt. Some dog beds fit comfortably inside a wire dog crate, especially the pillow type. However, do not use a pillow inside a crate for a puppy during housebreaking. A puppy just might chew the stuffing out of a pillow and swallow the material.

It is worth noting that in warm weather a Golden Retriever will prefer the cool surface of the floor or the smooth bottom of his wire crate. Older, arthritic dogs appreciate a large dog basket with a soft cushion in it, especially in cold weather.

Puppygate

Puppygate has nothing to do with political scandal. It is about keeping your dog out of trouble. Most dog trainers correctly advise their clients not to allow a puppy or untrained dog to have the run of the house when his family is too busy to watch him or when no one is home. An untrained puppy is certain to leave a mess to clean up after he relieves himself everywhere (they love carpets) in addition to getting into all kinds of trouble, such as chewing the furniture and whatever else he can sink his teeth into. *Confining a dog is an important aspect of housebreaking and paper training.* It is impossible to train most puppies to control themselves if they are *not* confined to one small area. A puppy gate does the job. See Chapter 7, "Housebreaking Your Golden Retriever."

If you confine your pet to one room and close the door, he will be isolated, which is an unnatural condition for all dogs. He will become bewildered, upset, lonely, and bored. A dog's response to being shut away is to bark, howl, and whine. In extreme cases isolation brings on *separation anxiety,* an abnormal fear of being left alone that can involve frantic attempts to escape, chewing the bottom off the door, clawing the walls, excessive elimination, all in addition to barking, howling, and whining. Do not isolate your dog. There is a better way.

Confining your puppy to a familiar room, such as the kitchen, is a healthier, happier solution and almost always avoids unpleasant behavior. Simply block the doorway with a puppy gate. It will allow the dog to watch everything that goes on in the other rooms and not feel isolated, even if no one is home. With the door to the room open and the gate attached, your puppy is able to see into the other rooms and feel less confined. Puppy (or child) gates are sold in hardware stores, pet supply stores and mail-order catalogs for pet owners. Highly recommended gates come in plastic-covered wood. Most of them work with a spring mechanism that applies pressure to each side of the doorway. Pet supply catalogs stock them in extra-wide sizes for special situations. Avoid accordion-type gates. As your Golden grows you will need two gates, one placed on top of the other, to prevent your dog from jumping over.

Collars

Puppies

Buy a soft, adjustable buckle or snap-together collar made of nylon, leather, or rolled leather. Experienced dog owners get inexpensive puppy collars at first because they must be replaced several times as the dog grows. A soft collar is necessary for a Golden Retriever so that it doesn't wear the hair off the neck. Check it daily for proper fit. There should be enough room for two fingers to slip in and out easily between the collar and the puppy's neck. It must not be too tight or too loose. *Attach an ID tag or one of the many ID products available to the collar with your home and work telephone numbers etched on it.*

Adult dogs

For everyday use, a simple, buckle collar made of nylon or cotton webbing with an ID tag attached is recommended. Some Golden Retriever breeders suggest nylon collars with a safety-release buckle and others suggest adjustable nylon collars. Rolled leather collars are also fine. Wide, flat leather collars are adequate but may wear away the hair around the neck. In addition, some leather collars stain the coat when wet.

Training collars

Training collars are also referred to as *choke collars*. This piece of equipment is essential for training dogs and solving behavior problems by allowing a mild correction to be administered with a tug of the leash. A metal training collar is recommended for a four-and-a-half-month-old Golden puppy if he is particularly stubborn and difficult to manage. However, do not use a metal training collar on a sensitive dog until he is at least six months or older.

A training collar is a rope of polished chain with a large metal ring at each end. Small rounded links are preferable. Nylon training collars are popular because they don't wear down a dog's coat. Metal collars are preferred because of their smooth, quick release after being tightened around the dog's neck. Training collars are also available in rolled leather but do not operate as smoothly as those made of metal links. See Chapter 8, "Obedience-Training Your Golden Retriever" for more information.

Size is an important consideration. Measure the circumference of your dog's neck by wrapping a tape measure around it. Add three inches to the measured width and buy a training collar of that length. Collars come in even-numbered sizes; if your measurement is an odd number, round up. If the collar is too long, it will make leash corrections less effective in addition to adding unnecessary weight for the dog to tote around.

A word of caution. Never leave an unsupervised puppy or grown dog with a training collar around his neck, not even if he is in a wire crate. That can be a safety hazard.

Leashes

A puppy's first leash

In order to develop a loving, well-behaved dog you must be able to control him, and that involves attaching a leash to his collar. All puppies must be introduced to the idea of wearing a leash as well as having their movements controlled by the person holding the leash. Some dogs have an easier time with this than others. Before attempting to use a leash on a puppy, dog trainers recommend an adjustment process called "leash breaking." See Leash Breaking in Chapter 8, "Obedience-Training Your Golden Retriever."

The all-purpose leash for grown dogs

Most dog trainers and breeders recommend a quality latigo leather leash three-fourths inch wide and six feet long with a brass-bolt snap for Golden Retrievers. This is the ideal leash for everyday use as well as for obedience training.

Some breeders prefer leashes made of nylon or cotton webbing for puppies and grown dogs. Leashes made of plastic or metal chain are not recommended. There is a consensus among experienced dog people that a six-foot leather leash is the safest, most durable type for training and everyday use. Leather softens with age, making it easier on the human hand, and it lasts longer than most other materials.

When a leather leash begins to wear, it develops thin sections, making it obvious that it needs to be replaced. This is important. If a weakened leash breaks when you are outdoors, your dog may bolt from you into traffic. Strength and comfort are the main considerations when selecting the proper leash for your dog.

Toys

Toys are thought of as objects designed for fun and entertainment. Toys for dogs, however, can be more than that. The right toys can prevent boredom and anxiety, which often lead to destructive behavior. Some toys help establish and reinforce the human-animal bond. Toys can also alleviate mild physical discomforts such as teething, as well as promote development of the dog's mind and body.

Puppyhood and canine adolescence entail the development of the physical and mental ability to survive. Nature provides a learning

All tired out after a round of play with a favorite toy.

process for this that includes various aspects of play behavior. A puppy or young dog's play promotes physical development, use of excess energy, establishment of territory or social rank, hunting for food, and maneuvers for getting out of threatening situations. Golden Retrievers' play usually has something to do with their instinct to hunt and retrieve. All of these elements can be seen by observing a litter of Golden puppies piling into a heap, wrestling, pawing each other, and carrying objects around in their mouth as they roll and tumble with amusing exuberance.

Toys for your new dog should promote exercise, relieve boredom, alleviate the discomfort of teething, or provide him with an outlet for his various urges and desires. The best toys appeal to a dog's basic instincts. When playing, dogs learn to develop the skills that are necessary to survive in the wild, as though they were wolves. When a puppy plays ball, he is actually learning to chase and capture something.

Plastic flying disks (Frisbees) when tossed are wonderful for establishing a bond between a dog and members of his family as well as satisfying many of the dog's instinctive urges. Tossing a disk or ball high into the air, though, is not recommended for puppies because of their soft joints, which may become injured as a result of jumping too high.

Because Golden Retrievers love stuffed toys, furry dog toys that squeak are highly recommended. They have no glass eyes or noses to swallow and do no damage when tossed around. Also recommended are the rubbery hive-shaped toys that bounce and roll in unexpected directions when tossed, as well as the latest generation of large, hard balls made of cressite rubber. These toys are not recommended for indoor use because of the physical action involved. Tennis balls are not suitable toys because they are small enough to swallow whole and lodge in a Golden Retriever's throat, causing a life-threatening situation. They can also be chewed into dangerous chunks that can be swallowed.

Teething is an irritating and sometimes painful stage for puppies and young dogs. Appropriate chew toys can help satisfy the urge to chew without harming the dog or his family's possessions. Although rawhide chew toys (usually shaped like bones) are acceptable, bone-shaped toys made of hard nylon material are superior because they require more effort to gnaw down and make little or no demand on the digestive system. When properly used, they can be an effective aid in solving destructive chewing problems.

For dog toys to be safe they must be well constructed and not easily destroyed. Dog owners can prevent medical problems by discarding old or half-chewed toys before pieces can be swallowed. No toy should be small enough to swallow. Avoid toys containing toxic materials, such as lead-based paint. Do not buy items with small parts that can be chewed off and swallowed, such as metal bells or rivets. Remove strings and ribbons.

If you purchase a chew toy that simulates something real in your home such as a shoe or a book, you run the risk of teaching your dog to chew the real thing. Reject all manner of pulling games. Games and toys that involve any version of tug-of-war stimulate the aggressive aspects of dog behavior and can lead to nipping, growling, and biting.

Grooming Tools

Brushes

Every puppy or adult dog needs a brush. A high-quality *pin brush* is the primary grooming tool needed for the care of the Golden Retriever coat. The one you select should be based on your dog's size as well as the length of the hair and its density. Consult a groomer or pet supplies dealer. Most Golden breeders recommend a pin brush as the primary grooming tool because it does not tear the coat or scratch the skin. A pin brush is made of many stainless-steel or chrome-plated pins with rounded ends that run through the coat like the bristles of a conventional brush. Better pin brushes have rubber-tipped pins set in a soft, foam-rubber base, which makes them very flexible. The pins come in short, medium, and long lengths and are selected on the basis of the length of a dog's coat.

Grooming a Golden Retriever also requires a *slicker brush* from time to time. The slicker brush is an odd-looking tool that is rectangular in shape, with a long handle and short, bent-wire teeth usually set in foam rubber. The metal teeth are like no others seen on a brush. This highly useful tool can be obtained in small, medium, and large sizes. It is used only for matted coats. If used regularly like any other brush, it will break the coat hair and cause *brush burn*, which is an inflammation of the skin. The sole purpose of the slicker brush is to untangle mats and remove dead hair, which is a necessary procedure for Golden Retrievers.

Combs

A fully grown Golden requires a large-size stainless-steel comb that is identified by groomers and breeders as a half-medium, half-fine comb. This comb is used for most medium- and long-haired breeds and coat types. Only the size varies from breed to breed. The fine teeth are for combing soft or silky hair; the medium teeth are for combing longer, thicker parts of the coat. Combs that are Teflon-coated at the tips add ease and smoothness to combing out a dog. Some Golden breeders and exhibitors also use a metal comb with wide teeth for combing out the *feathers*, which are the longer hairs that plume out on the ears, tail, underbelly, and legs.

You may at some time require the use of a *flea comb*. Although a flea comb does exactly what its name implies, it is not used exclusively to remove fleas. It is also useful for combing out facial and leg hair. Flea combs are very fine-tooth combs that come with or without handles.

Other grooming tools and supplies that are necessary for your Golden Retriever are a guillotine-type nail trimmer; a canine toothbrush; canine shampoo formulated for the Golden Retriever's coat texture; distilled water in a spray bottle or anti-static coat spray for brushing; a hose-type spray (for baths); a blow dryer (for after baths); ear cleaner; cotton balls; a grooming table (optional); powdered coagulant to stop nails from bleeding when clipped too close to the quick.

Coming home with a new puppy is like bringing a newborn baby into the house. Like any new mother and father you must provide the youngster with everything it will need, from food to love to learning how to behave. It is the normal order of things

If you treat your puppy as a new baby and take care of his needs, you won't go wrong. All of the gear discussed in this chapter will help ease the transition for everyone, but especially for the newest member of your family. If your new dog has not yet arrived, then buy the things the dog needs beforehand. If the dog is already enjoying your hospitality, then go out and get the things recommended. It is never too late. It all goes to make the first day and *all* the days that follow as wonderful as possible.

CHAPTER SIX

Feeding Your Dog

Feeding a dog, from puppyhood to old age, is of enormous importance and is one of the areas in which dog owners can significantly influence their pets' health and well-being. Because of continuing advances in nutritional science, the pet food industry has been able to make it easy for everyone to properly feed their dogs. Through extensive research, pet food manufacturers have learned how to formulate dog foods so that they provide the required nutrients in correct proportions for growth, day-to-day maintenance, pregnancy, lactation, hard work, and various stressful conditions, such as cold weather or extreme emotions.

When prey animals are plentiful, wolves (or dogs) living in the wild get a complete and balanced diet by eating what they hunt, which is usually grass-eating herbivores. The first part of a kill that is eaten is the viscera and the stomach contents, which, along with the bones and muscle meat, provide carbohydrates, vitamins, minerals, and fiber, all needed to create a complete and balanced diet. Companion animals living in our homes must also obtain the same high level of nourishment as their cousins in the wild if they are to live long and healthy lives. In order to achieve this goal, dog owners must feed their pets a proper diet. Feeding a dog a complete and balanced diet will make life easier for the family and healthier for the dog.

In the wild, wolves (or dogs) must search for their food to survive. They hunt in packs and eat the prey animals they are able to capture. With that accomplished, they consume as much as they possibly can in one meal because they cannot be sure when they will eat again. This seemingly gluttonous behavior is the source of the expression "wolfing down your food."

It is a fact that Golden Retrievers love to eat as much as they love to do anything, perhaps more. However, if you compare the behavioral and medical difficulties of finicky dogs that refuse to eat, overeating is easier to cope with. Still, a Golden Retriever can eat itself into unattractive obesity, serious health problems, and a shortened life span if its family allows it to happen. The problem is not what the dog eats. The problem is what the dog is fed. It is the pet owner's obligation to control the quality and quantity of a dog's diet.

Food For Thought

High-quality, brand-name commercial dog foods are recommended for Golden Retrievers by most breeders and professional dog people. These contain quality ingredients with all the essential nutritional requirements of dogs in addition to being highly digestible and palatable. Commercial dog foods are made in several forms and vary in their moisture content, shape, density, texture, and ingredients. Convenience, palatability, cost, and the quality of the food are the deciding factors when selecting one commercial product from the other.

Some people prefer to feed their dogs preparations made in their own kitchens. To do this properly requires a knowledge of the minimum daily requirements of dogs and the precise nutritional ratios of protein, carbohydrate, fat, vitamins, and minerals. When these nutritional essentials are ignored or unknown, a wide assortment of health problems may result. At their best, homemade meals for dogs are carefully formulated and fed with regard to the dog's minimum daily requirements. At their worst, home-cooked meals consist of table scraps and leftovers, haphazardly fed to the dog for the sake of convenience, cost, and avoidance of waste. No breeder, handler, veterinarian, or other professional dog person advocates this approach to feeding dogs.

Superior commercial dog food is available in supermarkets, pet food shops, feed stores, or from veterinarians. It can be obtained in three forms: dry food, canned food, and semimoist food.

Dry dog food

These grain or cereal types are packaged as meals, pellets, biscuits, kibbles (broken biscuits), or expanded products. The hard-baked biscuits are usually shaped like bones.

The average dry dog food contains approximately 1,500 calories per pound. It includes 10 percent moisture. Cereal grains are the primary ingredients of dry dog foods in addition to soybean products, milk products, vitamin and mineral supplements, various animal protein sources, and fats and oils (sprayed on the surface for palatability). Most dogs are attracted to quality dry dog food. However, it is more appealing when the food is substantially moistened. Dogs will eat approximately 20 percent more when water or other liquid has been added.

Dry food costs less money than other types of food, is more convenient, and does not spoil as quickly as canned food. Manufacturers of brand-name dry dog food claim that their products do not require vitamin and mineral supplements. Most veterinarians agree. Dry dog food has become the most popular dog food used.

Canned dog food

The main feature of canned dog food is its very high moisture content, which averages between 74 and 78 percent.

Canned dog foods are produced in two general forms: 1. the canned meat type, which contains mostly meat and poultry along with their by-products, fat, a small quantity of soy products, plus added vitamins and minerals; 2. mixed or standard canned ration, which contains large quantities of cereal grains, soybean products, fat, meat and meat by-products, plus vitamin and mineral supplements.

Most canned dog foods provide complete nutrition and can be fed exclusively. Canned foods are appealing to dogs because of their abundant water and fat content, which affects smell, taste, and appearance. They contain between 500 and 600 calories per 14- to 15-ounce can depending on the brand, the size, and the contents. Some dog owners use canned foods exclusively; others add them as a flavoring to dry food in small amounts or restrict them to a transitional diet for puppies being weaned from mother's milk to solid food. Feeding a growing Golden canned food exclusively is expensive.

Semimoist foods

Semimoist food has the appearance of ground or cubed meat in color, texture, and shape. It contains 25 to 30 percent moisture and provides between 1,350 and 1,500 calories per pound. This food type contains animal products (meat and meat by-products), milk products, fats and oils, soybean products, and mineral and vitamin supplements. Semimoist dog food is complete and balanced and may be fed as the primary diet.

Some dog owners use semimoist food as a supplement to other types of foods, including homemade meals. It is odorless to humans but attractive and highly palatable to dogs. This type of dog food requires no refrigeration and comes in premeasured portions. It has a high sugar content and costs considerably more than dry food. Feeding your Golden a diet consisting of semimoist food exclusively during housebreaking training is undesirable as it tends to increase a dog's water intake, which in turn increases the dog's frequency of urination.

Dog biscuits and snacks

Manufactured dog biscuits are another form of dry dog food. They have high nutritional value and can be used as part of a dog's daily diet. Check the label to be sure that the biscuits are consistent with the ingredients of high-quality dog food. Hard-baked biscuits (usually shaped like bones) as well as other types of snacks have become quite popular as rewards for good behavior and expressions of affection.

Snack products are used to supplement the dog's usual diet and are given as an expression of love and approval. Some pet owners use commercial snack foods as part of their dogs' diet, but most veterinarians believe this is not essential.

When used sparingly as treats, these food products serve to strengthen and promote the bond between dogs and their families. They are also used by some dog trainers as a reward for good performance.

The ingredients of these foods vary widely in their nutritional value. Generally speaking, they are often higher in salt, fat, and sugar content and are not recommended as a total dog ration. Snacks should not represent more than 10 percent of your dog's daily food intake.

Feeding a Balanced Diet

When selecting a commercial dog food for your Golden Retriever, it is desirable to choose one that is labeled "Complete and Balanced" or words to that effect. Dog foods on the shelves of supermarkets and pet food shops may or may not offer this important advantage. Such labeling indicates that the ingredients of the product are not only of high quality but are combined in the proper proportions and contain the necessary nutrients to satisfy a dog's established energy requirements.

A number of variables determine how much to feed a dog and, to some degree, what to feed (more or less protein or fat, for example). The nutritional requirements of dogs vary depending on age, metabolism, activity level, and lifestyle.

Adult dogs living as pets do not require as much food as dogs in other stages of life or in exceptional situations. The intensive-growth period of puppies, for example (eight weeks to twelve months), creates the need for them to consume more food than at any other time in their lives. Consequently, growing puppies require more calories per pound of body weight than adult dogs. Pregnant females or those nursing a litter of puppies require more food because of the greater demands made on their bodies. Hard-working, active dogs, such as field dogs or protection dogs, cannot survive without the added energy from greater quantities of food with increased fat content, especially if they are outdoors in cold weather. Dogs that are physically or emotionally stressed also need to be fed more food than usual to maintain their health. *Do not rely on general statements when deciding about your Golden's diet. Ask your dog's breeder, veterinarian, or professional trainer to help you determine what to feed your dog and in what specific amount.*

Feeding Guidelines for Golden Retrievers

Most breeders and experienced Golden owners feed their dogs a high-quality, dry dog food with a high fat and protein content. How much to feed a dog depends on many factors, as noted above. A healthy dog's appetite is based on his energy requirements.

Puppies become fully grown dogs slightly before or slightly after their second birthday. The quantity of food eaten diminishes dramatically as they approach adulthood. Young dogs tell you when to reduce the quantity of food by leaving much of it in the bowl. If a puppy eats all the food in his bowl for three days in a row, increase the amount slightly. If food is left in the bowl for three days in a row, decrease the amount slightly.

A healthy Golden Retriever puppy getting proper nutrition maintains a steady rate of growth, a full, glossy coat, and a slight thickness of fat beneath the skin.

As an adult your Golden will require a consistent diet that offers no more or less than his lifestyle requires. Although he will require fewer calories per pound than he did as a puppy, he may require more food than he did as a puppy simply because he weighs more.

Establish your dog's ideal or desired body weight (with the help of a breeder or a veterinarian). Feed him a high-quality ration that will maintain the established body weight. Initially, weigh your dog once a week to determine if the food is adding or subtracting body weight. If his weight fluctuates by more than 10 percent from the established ideal weight, adjust the ration by feeding him more or less food.

The nutritional requirements of two dogs of the same age and weight, even from the same litter of puppies, may vary as much as 100 percent; one dog may require twice as much food as the other. Once you determine how much to feed, check the dog's weight once a month to be sure you are able to maintain his ideal weight. Always measure the amount of food you give your dog. Do not estimate the amount.

How to weigh your dog

First, weigh yourself on a bathroom scale. Second, hold the dog in your arms and weigh yourself again. Subtract the first figure from the second figure to determine your dog's exact weight.

Amounts of food

It is difficult to make a general statement about exact amounts of food because of the differences in nutritional requirements from one dog to another. When deciding how much to feed your adult dog, use this handy shortcut: one pound of premium dry food will feed approximately 60 pounds of dog per day.

One can of high-quality dog food will feed approximately 20 pounds of dog per day (based on 500 calories per 20 pounds). A 60 pound dog, therefore, will require approximately three cans per day.

One patty of semimoist food is approximately equal to one half can of dog food. Thus, one patty will feed approximately 10 pounds of dog per day. A 60 pound dog will require 6 semimoist patties per day.

These generalized amounts are merely guidelines for average dogs living average lives. Each dog must be evaluated on an individual basis, taking into consideration the differences in metabolic rate, size, temperament, environment, and work routine, if any. Consult a veterinarian for more specific instructions concerning your own dog.

Feeding Premium Dry Food

(Amounts given are for the typical house dog's maintenance and not for working, pregnant, or performance dogs. Consult a veterinarian.)

Puppies (weaned to eight weeks)
Feed three-fourths cup dry food *four times a day. It is important to soak dry food in the bowl.*

Puppies (eight weeks to six months)
Feed one cup dry food *three times a day* (depending on age, size, and activity level). *It is important to soak dry food in the bowl.* Some three-month-old puppies or older puppies may refuse their midday meal. Add the food to the morning and evening meals. If the young dog leaves food in the bowl, eliminate one cup (more or less) from the daily ration.

Adults (one year and older)
Feed two cups of dry food *twice a day. It is important to soak dry food in the bowl.*

Pour water, soup, or, if it is tolerated, whole or evaporated milk in the bowl, enough to barely cover the food, and let it sit for fifteen minutes before feeding it to the dog. The food will absorb most of the liquid and resemble a meat-type ration.

It is important to soak dry food because Golden Retrievers, like most large dogs, are vulnerable to a life-threatening medical condition known as bloat or gastric dilation-volvulus.

Veterinarians recommend soaking dry food in a liquid for fifteen minutes before feeding it to the dog. The liquid expands the food in the bowl rather than in the dog's stomach, possibly reducing the creation of intestinal gas. This in turn reduces the risk of bloat. Soaking the food may even slow down ravenous eating behavior.

Many experienced owners and breeders feed their Goldens a premium-quality dry food with a high fat content. Some mix the dry ration with canned food.

Premium dog foods formulated for "puppies" or "growth" are used by some breeders but not by others, who believe that puppy foods accelerate weight gain and the rate of growth and that along with improper exercise they can create orthopedic problems.

Although supplemental foods and snacks are not necessary, they are as pleasing for the owner to give as they are for the dog to receive. Supplemental foods, however, should be healthful and nutritious. As a special health treat we recommend that you occasionally indulge your Golden Retriever with small quantities of cottage cheese, plain yogurt, scrambled eggs, fruits and vegetables (cooked or raw) such as grapes, apples, green beans, or carrots. Among the most often-used food treats that Goldens love are dog biscuits, which can be offered as a reward or gesture of approval. Added foods may be given before, after, during, or between meals but in small portions.

All breeders agree that Goldens are easy to feed. They'll eat everything and beg for more if you permit it. Do not overfeed them, especially puppies. There is a consensus among Golden Retriever people that a breed prone to hip dysplasia, such as this one, must not become too big too soon. (See Chapter 12, "Medical Problems Common to the Golden Retriever.")

Do not feed your dog chocolate of any kind (it is toxic to dogs), raw eggs (they are difficult to digest, and raw egg white is especially harmful), raw meat or fish (they may be contaminated by dangerous internal parasites).

Some Goldens become obsessed with food, especially as they get older. Dog owners should know that it's okay if their pets are a bit leaner than those in the show ring.

Overweight Dogs

To determine if your dog is overweight feel around his chest. Run your palm along the ribs on each side. A healthy, normal dog should not retain very much fat between the skin and the ribs. A dog of normal weight will have a thin layer of fat covering the rib cage, enough for a slight finger indentation when pressed. One-fifth of an inch of tissue covering the ribs is the appropriate thickness. If the shape of the ribs cannot be seen, the dog is probably obese. Fat protrusions are obvious, particularly under the stomach or chin or on torsos that resemble a rounded, shapeless cylinder from neck to tail. These are the conditions of an obese dog. Excluding medical conditions, overweight is the result of consuming more calories (from too much food) than are needed to grow, reproduce, or function.

Because Goldens do most of their growing within the first twelve to eighteen months of life, they require more food during this period than at any other time in their lives. This is often misinterpreted by pet owners as the animal's normal food intake. When the dog suddenly stops eating large amounts, the owner believes he is sick and rewards him with love and affection for eating more than he wants. Unfortunately, these good intentions harm the family pet's health by creating an association of food with love and approval. Food should be nothing more or less than the source of life-sustaining nutrition.

◆ ◆ ◆

Housebreaking Your Golden Retriever

All Golden Retrievers can and should be housebroken. Fortunately, this breed accepts housebreaking quite easily and has no problems with the techniques. Only those with medical problems have any difficulties, and even they can be housebroken when the medical problem is corrected. A puppy of eight weeks and older can begin this program and be housebroken within one week. Depending upon the dog, the owners, and consistent adherence to the program, the average Golden can be housebroken in three days to three weeks. Young puppies will still require confinement after they have been housebroken until they're proven reliable, which will be at four or five months of age.

Housebreaking means your Golden Retriever is trained to urinate and defecate *outdoors* on a schedule of your choosing based on your needs. The dog must *always* relieve himself in a convenient location outdoors. He must *always* control himself until he can be taken out. The dog is never allowed to relieve himself indoors.

Housebreaking is not paper training and has nothing to do with the use of newspapers on the floor. Housebreaking is the only sensible option because it is not practical to paper-train Golden Retrievers. They are large dogs that eliminate in great quantities. Paper training and housebreaking involve methods that are similar in some aspects but quite different in others. These two methods of training have conflicting objectives. Housebreaking is the only technique recommended for Golden Retrievers.

Many novice dog owners use newspapers on the floor as a temporary measure until their puppy is able to go outside. Some puppies and adult dogs are encouraged to eliminate on newspapers, indoors as well as on the ground. Doing both prolongs housebreaking with only marginal success. Utilizing both methods tends to confuse the dog, causing "accidents" and "mistakes."

Eliminating over newspapers teaches a dog to relieve himself on your floor and to claim (and constantly reclaim) territory in your home by marking it with the scent of his urine and feces. This is called *scent marking*. Some dogs scent-post many places in your home. It is difficult for them to confine this instinctive behavior to one spot on the floor after they have been encouraged to use newspapers. Paper training teaches dogs to use the floor.

The best situation is to begin housebreaking your puppy the minute he comes to live with you, ideally at eight weeks of age. This may conflict with instructions from your veterinarian, who advises you to keep your young dog indoors until he gets all his vaccinations; this may not be accomplished until the puppy is four months old. We do not suggest that you ignore your veterinarian's advice. However, you must understand that allowing your puppy to relieve himself on newspapers before getting him to go outdoors, without soiling in your house, causes behavioral confusion. The changeover will take longer and demand greater effort and patience on your part.

Procedures and Technique for Housebreaking

The elements of this housebreaking program are 1. the feed-water-walk schedule, 2. feeding your dog during housebreaking, 3. removing odors of past mistakes, 4. confinement, and 5. correction and praise. These elements will work only when used together. To leave any one or more of them out during the housebreaking process will ensure failure. All aspects of the five-part program are valid for the life of the dog, with the exception of confinement.

1. The Feed-Water-Walk Schedule

Dogs living indoors benefit most from a schedule regulating their food, water, and elimination. The object is to condition the dog's mind and body to eliminating body waste at specific times of the day and night. Daily repetition of feeding, drinking, and walking at the same times creates in the dog's mind and body a timing mechanism that will last a lifetime. Depending upon the size of the dog, his age, the amount he eats, and his house training, it will take three to six hours after feeding for the food to travel through his digestive system and leave his body. Obviously, puppies digest food much sooner than grown dogs. By learning your dog's digestion time, you can predict when he must relieve himself. The schedule must be adjusted to suit other physical needs as well. For example, puppies, with smaller bladders and stomachs and immature sphincter muscles, must be walked more frequently than mature dogs. Because eating and drinking stimulates elimination (peristalsis) most dogs relieve themselves immediately after eating. Consult your veterinarian for your dog's digestion time.

By always feeding, watering, and walking your dog at the same times every day, you teach him to create an inner schedule consistent with your schedule. This inner schedule will continue after the housebreaking program is finished. The dog becomes motivated to control his need to eliminate because his body clock anticipates walks at specific times every day.

Bear in mind that a dog's age determines the type of schedule you create for him. A young dog must be fed more often than a fully grown dog. During the major growth period (three to ten months of age), puppies require more food per pound of body weight than older dogs do. They should not eat their entire daily ration at one meal. They need to eliminate more frequently, and that means more walks. Young puppies should be walked according to the schedule opposite.

Mature dogs do not need as many walks (for the purpose of elimination) as younger, smaller dogs. They can control their need to relieve themselves for much longer periods of time.

When you are setting up a feed-water-walk schedule, the first walk of the day should be determined by how many hours have passed since the dog was last walked. *There must not be a nighttime interval longer than eight hours.* If your dog's last walk was at 11:00 P.M., his first walk the next morning should be at 7:00 A.M. Here are some suggested schedules that can be used exactly as they are or adjusted to take into account the needs of your dog or your family.

Schedule for Puppies Two to Six Months Old

7:00 A.M.	Walk the dog.
7:30 A.M.	Feed, water, and walk.
11:30 A.M.	Feed, water, and walk.
4:30 P.M.	Feed, water, and walk.
8:30 P.M.	Water and walk (last water of the day).
11:00 P.M.	Walk the dog.

Schedule for Dogs Six Months to One Year Old

7:00 A.M.	Walk the dog.
7:30 A.M.	Feed, water, and walk.
12:30 P.M.	Water and walk.
4:30 P.M.	Feed, water, and walk.
7:30 P.M.	Water and walk (last water of the day).
11:00 P.M.	Walk the dog.

Schedule for Dogs One Year Old and Older

7:00 A.M.	Walk the dog.
7:30 A.M.	Feed, water, and walk.
4:30 P.M.	Water and walk.
7:30 P.M.	Water and walk (last water of the day).
11:00 P.M.	Walk the dog.

Schedule for Those Who Go to Work

First thing in the morning	Walk the dog.
Before leaving for work	Feed, water, and walk.

Midday	Have a neighbor or hired walker feed, water, and walk a puppy (only water and walk a grown dog).
Home from work	Walk the dog.
Immediately after walk	Feed, water, and walk a puppy or dog under one year old (only water and walk a grown dog).
Early evening	Water and walk (last water of the day).
Before going to bed	Walk the dog.

When walking your new dog or puppy for the first time, bear in mind your pet's need to or mark or scent his own territory with his urine. This instinct works to your advantage. Allow your dog to seek out the scent marks of other dogs and eliminate over them. These will become permanent stations along the path of your dog's daily walks. Congratulate and praise your dog every time he relieves himself anyplace outdoors. An important part of the teaching process is to praise him for doing the right thing and correct him when he does the wrong thing.

2. Feeding Your Dog During Housebreaking

Meeting your dog's nutritional requirements should always be the first consideration when selecting a proper diet. However, during the housebreaking period there is another equally important goal. It is essential that the dog's digestion be in perfect order or the housebreaking program will fail. If your dog develops loose stools, diarrhea, or the need to urinate excessively, it will be impossible for him to follow any of the feed-water-walk schedules and he will not become trained.

Feed your dog his normal ration as recommended in Chapter 6, "Feeding Your Dog." Moistened dry dog food is highly recommended to maintain a firm stool and allow for successful housebreaking. Do not overfeed your dog. However, puppies must be allowed to eat as much as they want for growth. If your dog leaves food in the bowl or is defecating excessively, you are feeding him too much. Reduce his food portion. Do not feed your dog between-meal snacks or leftovers from the table. Adhere to the feeding schedule with great consistency.

Your dog's stomach is sensitive. Any sudden changes in his diet will cause diarrhea, and that will bring the housebreaking process to a halt. If you are going to change your dog's diet, do not make the switch suddenly. Hold off on housebreaking until the change is completed. Over a four-day period, add one-fourth new food to three-fourths of the old food, increasing the amount by fourths each time as you decrease the old food by the same amount. Once you have settled all the questions about your dog's diet, you may begin the housebreaking program.

3. Removing Odors of Past Mistakes

A dog's scenting ability is the greatest of all his senses. Picture the human nose and then compare it to the canine muzzle. Inside each is a fine lining that is a membrane containing thousands of smell receptors (in humans) and millions of receptors (in dogs). In humans this area is less than one inch long. In dogs it can be four inches long. Smells trigger electric impulses to the olfactory center in the brain, arriving there as raw information to be evaluated. Dogs use their noses more than their eyes and maintain a memory storage in the brain based on smells. The canine sense of smell is extraordinary.

It is impossible to housebreak a dog unless you obliterate all past odors of his own urine and defecation. This includes past mistakes on the carpet and areas of the floor where he was permitted to use newspapers as a toilet. Every time the dog relieves himself on the floor, an odor remains no matter how well you may scrub it away. This remaining odor draws the dog back to that spot and triggers his instinct to "mark" on top of it. It is a continuing cycle that can be ended only when the dog's scent of urine or feces is eliminated. This explains why dogs with housebreaking problems always seem to relieve themselves in the same locations. Although the odor may not be evident to the human nose, it is perceptible to the intricate smell mechanism of a dog's nose. Buy an odor neutralizer concentrate at a pet supply store or mail-order catalog and use it according to instructions. This type of product is the only means available to obliterate previous scent posts in your house successfully. Ammonia, bleach, vinegar, and other household products do not mask the odors of body waste from the dog's keen sense of smell. Odor neutralizers do not remove or perfume the smells; they alter them. (It is important to note that ammonia intensifies the odor of urine and tends to attract animals rather than repel them.)

4. Confinement

Puppies that are not housebroken will relieve themselves about every hour (depending on their activity level and water intake) and will do it on the floor, in front of you. Adolescent and mature dogs who have experienced your displeasure have greater sphincter control and will wait until you leave before letting go on the carpet. It is not defiance, arrogance, spite, or stupidity that makes them behave this way. They are simply unhousebroken dogs caught in the crossfire between human demands and their natural inclinations. Their bodies have not been regulated and they have not been taught (in a manner they can understand) what you expect of them.

Restricting your dog's indoor movements (especially when no one is home) is a key factor for a successful housebreaking program. During the housebreaking program, confine your dog or puppy if you do not have time to watch for the signs that tell you he is going to relieve himself. (Dogs and puppies sniff close to the ground, whimper and whine, make gagging sounds, turn in circles, and even head for the door when they must eliminate.) If you are going to leave the house, it is essential that the dog in the housebreaking program be confined to one small area of your home until you return.

Dogs are born with the instinct not to soil their eating and sleeping area. They are also taught this by their mothers. When you confine your dog, he quickly realizes that he will be forced to remain in the same area with his urine and feces if he lets go. Sometimes a dog cannot help himself and soils his own area anyway. However, he has not soiled the entire house, creating more aggravation (and scent areas to return to).

Do not mistake "confinement" for imprisonment or tying the dog down someplace. Simply confine the dog in a small but comfortable area adequate for his physical and psychological needs. Leave him in the selected confinement area with his food, water, toys, and bedding. A puppy gate installed in the doorway will keep him there. Double gates (one placed on top of the other) are necessary for grown dogs so that they cannot jump over.

The kitchen is the most commonly chosen confinement site because of the size, location, and floor covering. Linoleum or floor tiles will withstand your dog's "accidents" better than any other covering. This is the ideal situation. You may also use a bathroom or small hallway for this purpose. The area should be large enough for the dog to walk around without feeling punished, and he should be able to see other parts of the house and family activities.

Never confine your dog or puppy behind a closed door. This is psychologically harmful and counterproductive. Some owners have successfully housebroken their dogs using the same wire dog crates purchased for other confinement purposes. Many breeders recommend them, although they are not necessary for housebreaking unless you have no other practical area for confinement. Choose a wire dog crate that is the correct size for your dog with enough room for him to stand up and turn around in. It can serve as a confinement area providing the dog is not left in it for an entire day.

During the housebreaking program, confine your dog when you leave the house or do not have time to watch for his mistakes. *Do not lay any newspapers down on the floor in the confinement area*. If the dog has an accident on the floor, take him outside and praise him lavishly if he eliminates there. Clean up the mess from the floor, get rid of the scent with an odor neutralizer, and continue the program as outlined. Using newspapers on the floor only teaches the dog to use the floor and prevents the successful conclusion to housebreaking.

It is good for the dog to run around loose as much as possible. Release him from confinement when you get home. The dog should be allowed to run around in the house, provided that someone watches him for signs that he has to relieve himself.

5. Correction and Praise

This is the fifth element of housebreaking, the most important part of the program. If your dog relieves himself inside the house in front of you, rattle a shake can vigorously and say, "NO," in a loud, firm voice to impress him with your displeasure. To make a shake can, take an empty soda can, wash it, and insert ten pennies into it. Tape the opening so the pennies cannot fall out. Shake the can vigorously. It will make a very loud, commanding rattle similar to the sound of a New Year's Eve noisemaker. It is an effective way to correct a dog, especially a puppy. It easily gets his attention when shaken loudly. It enables you to deliver a correction from across the room without the use of a leash. However, the manner in which you say, "NO," should be based on your dog's sensitivity. A puppy or overly sensitive dog cannot tolerate an overbearing manner or even a shake can too vigorously rattled. You do not want to terrorize your dog. You simply want to get his attention and deliver a corrective reprimand.

Your dog will probably stop eliminating if your correction was firm enough (for his personality). Place a leash and choke collar on him and quickly take him outside to the place where he is supposed to relieve himself. Praise him the minute you get there, whether he relieves himself or not. If he continues to eliminate in the correct area, lavish him with tremendous praise. This praise and correction is an important element of the teaching process. Place several shake cans around the house for warning and keep the dog's leash and choke collar handy. If you cannot reach a shake can in time say, "NO," in a loud, firm tone of voice and then take the dog out. Praise him afterward.

The only language that communicates between dogs and humans is the one of positive and negative messages. It is precisely how dogs communicate between themselves. Dogs thrive on acceptance and praise. When these are denied and negative messages are substituted, most dogs correct their behavior. It is the only known teaching process available for domestic dogs.

The most common misconception that dog owners have is the meaning of the term "correction." It is often confused with the word "punishment." Punishment is a penalizing act for wrongdoing that involves harsh or painful treatment. In dog training, a correction is different. A correction is nothing more than a negative message to a dog that he was incorrect or did not behave properly. Corrections must be humane and nonabusive in order to preserve the pleasant relationship between dog and human as well as teach in a positive way.

Punishing a dog for destructive behavior, for example, may offer a temporary emotional release, but it teaches a dog nothing except to fear you. *Punishment is not teaching.* If your dog misbehaves, your objective should be to solve the problem, not to punish the dog. These are two different matters.

Corrections, or negative messages, are simple, humane techniques for communicating to a dog that he has done the wrong thing. The *corrective jerk* is the most effective and most frequently used correction technique available to dog owners. It delivers a mild, negative sensation with the use of a leash and choke collar. It must not be performed in a manner that hurts the dog. The reason dogs interpret it as a negative message is that it is always accompanied with the verbal reprimand "NO." The jerk of the leash and the slight tightening of the choke collar (for an instant) are associated with the owner's criticism and lack of approval. The correction is part of the teaching process.

Praise is a reward. It motivates a dog to do whatever it is that you expect of him. You should always praise him for his efforts. If he misbehaves or fails to execute a command, correct him with the corrective jerk, the rattle of a shake can, or by saying, "NO," in a firm tone of voice. *After every correction it is essential that you immediately praise your dog.* It reassures him and rewards him for trying to do the right thing.

Do not correct your dog for messing in the house unless you catch him in the act. Your dog has no way of associating your correction with a house-soiling "accident" if it happened more than ten seconds before you discovered it. Correcting him later would be useless and unkind. Never yell, hit, swat with a newspaper, or rub your dog's nose in his own mess. It is unthinkable to hit a child for making a mistake when you are teaching him or her something new. The same is true for a dog. Do not slap a newspaper against your hand as a correction. It threatens the dog and is simply a form of punishment. Your hands should only be associated with good things, such as expressions of affection. The objective is not to frighten the dog but to tell him that he has just done something wrong. The next step is to teach him the correct thing to do.

CHAPTER EIGHT

Obedience-Training Your Golden Retriever

Golden Retrievers are among the easiest breeds to teach. They are famous for their desire to please. Training a typical Golden puppy is fun for the dog and his family, and that attitude should be reflected every time you work with the dog. The essence of this dog training course involves love, praise, and corrections.

Obedience training is based on a dog's acceptance of the human's higher-ranking position and the animal's need to have someone leading his pack. In the training course offered here, the dog is rewarded with praise each time he carries out a command properly. He is corrected when he does not obey the command or perform it properly (*only after it has been taught to him*). This establishes the trainer as the leader of the dog's pack.

The Training Course

The training elements of SIT, SIT-STAY, HEEL and automatic SIT, DOWN, DOWN-STAY, and COME WHEN CALLED offered in this chapter encompass a complete basic obedience training course. We cover step-by-step details for teaching your dog each of the six basic commands. We also offer the proper use of praise and corrections as motivational techniques. These training elements will help you communicate with your dog on a meaningful level. Obedience training is the language of dogs and people and makes life better for everyone.

Training Sessions

Training puppies (seven weeks to six months)

A very young puppy (up to four or five months old) should not wear a training collar with which to be corrected. Young puppies will respond properly to gentle leash corrections with a regular collar. Use a leather or nylon collar with a buckle. Few, if any, puppies ever perform obedience commands with precision no matter what type of collar they wear.

Do not overwork a young puppy. Restricting sessions to ten minutes several times a day will prevent him from becoming bored. If the dog does something right, praise him and move on to something else. If you do not have the dog's attention, it means you are not making it fun. You may be pushing the puppy too hard or too long. This will only produce a bored and resentful dog and will not have a positive effect on you, either. Although obedience training is not playtime, it should not be hard work. It is important to make sure the puppy or young dog responds on the first command by placing him in position with your hands if necessary. Corrections should be gentle but firm, not harsh, and certainly not abusive.

Training adolescent dogs (six to eighteen months)

Adolescents are capable of longer sessions and greater precision than puppies. Take into account your dog's stamina, attention span, and personality. No two dogs are alike. If your Golden is obedient but is looking away or has lost his enthusiasm, then you have practiced too long. End your sessions with the successful completion of a command and before the dog loses interest.

After teaching each command, it is important to keep practicing it until the next session. By all means practice in the yard or in the house all the commands your dog has learned, letting him know that he must listen to you wherever he is and at all times. Throw commands such as "SIT-STAY" at the door, "SIT-STAY" for his food, and so on, into your everyday life.

Do not give commands to your dog while he is off-leash or in situations where you do not have control. This will encourage your puppy or young dog to disregard you and test your authority. The adolescent Golden is going to test you at some point, so early training requiring a consistent response is extremely important.

Training adult dogs (eighteen months and older)

Training the adult dog can be as much fun as training a puppy but with quicker results. It must still be fun but consistent, with fair corrections. Some adult Goldens have stubborn moments and can put their owners to the test. Do not train your dog if you are tired or in a bad mood. Skip it until you feel better. Goldens are sensitive and respond negatively to inappropriate or harsh human behavior. On the other hand, the ideal tonic for changing your mood and cheering yourself up may be a training session with your dog (or puppy).

Praise

In this training course rewarding your dog for obeying and performing properly comes in the form of verbal praise, usually as enthusiastic compliments such as, "Good girl. What a good dog!" At times an affectionate pat on the body makes an appropriate addition to the reward. Some dog trainers use food tidbits for this purpose, but it is not recommended here except in special situations.

When a dog is being obedience-trained he works for your praise as his reward. It tells him that you are pleased with his performance and reinforces the teaching of each command. Golden Retrievers work for your approval. Most Goldens are high-energy, outgoing dogs but not all. Some are moderate-tempered, somewhat insecure, less outgoing, or more sensitive than others.

High-energy Goldens should be praised each time they carry out a command properly but not to the extent that they become overly excited. If you are too enthusiastic with your praise, the dog will become extremely playful rather than attentive, and the training session will end. Moderate-tempered Goldens should be praised with cheerfulness and enthusiasm in order to make them secure and less hesitant.

Corrections

There is only one acceptable way to communicate to your dog that he did the wrong thing, and that is with a *correction*. A correction is a reprimand conveyed to the dog in a way that is not harsh, abusive, or angry. It is simply a negative message that is communicated with a leash and training collar and with the word "NO." A leash correction (see The Corrective Jerk, page 107) and a verbal correction ("NO!") are usually given at the same time, although verbal corrections alone are all that is necessary for a trained dog.

All Golden Retrievers are sensitive and cannot tolerate severe corrections, harsh verbal reprimands, or punishments. They do vary to some degree in temperament and personality, however. Most

Goldens are high-energy dogs and require a firm leash correction followed with moderate praise because they want to play, run, and jump most of the time. There are Goldens with moderate temperaments and they respond best to softer, gentler corrections with highly enthusiastic praise. When training your own dog, you will quickly learn by trial and error how firm to make your corrections and how energetic your praise should be in order to get the appropriate response from the dog.

The Training Collar and Leash

Before you are able to administer a leash correction or teach any of the commands, you must know how to use the training collar and leash. This involves the correct way to place the collar around the dog's neck and learning how to hold the leash properly.

Placing the Training Collar Around the Dog's Neck

Hold one end of the collar by the ring with your left hand. The length of chain will fall into a vertical line. Attach the leash to the top ring. Grasp the bottom ring with your right hand. Work the chain (or nylon) through the bottom ring so that it drops through, forming a wide loop. Gravity will help. Most of the chain will drop through the bottom ring, creating a loop that goes around the dog's neck like a lasso.

As you face the dog, place the loop around his neck. This must be done properly for the dog's comfort and to make the collar work correctly. *The collar must be capable of tightening around the dog's neck when pulled and loosening when it is released.* It must slide back and forth smoothly and quickly. This is essential.

When placing the training collar over the dog's head, it is correct if it resembles the letter *P* around his neck as you face him. It is incorrect if it resembles the number *9*. (*If the collar is put on incorrectly it will not tighten and release quickly and smoothly.*)

Once you have formed a wide loop, place the dog's head through with the rings on the right side. The collar is on correctly if it forms the letter P and tightens and releases smoothly and quickly.

Holding the Leash Properly

Stand next to the dog on his right side, facing in the same direction, so that you are both looking forward. At the end of every leather and nylon leash is a sewn loop serving as a handle. Hook the top of the loop onto your right thumb. As it hangs from your thumb across your palm, grab the middle of the leash with your left hand and fold it over the loop that is hooked around your right thumb. Four straps of leather will now lie across the palm of your right hand. Close your fingers around them so they are pointing toward you. Adjust the length of the leash so that it crosses the width of your body, allowing a little slack.

For added strength, grip the leash with *both* hands as if holding a baseball bat. Place your left hand directly under the right one. This will allow you to jerk the leash effectively when correcting your dog. Maintain a relaxed but firm grip. Keep your hands close to the center of your body, slightly above or below the waist (whichever is more comfortable). The grip described above will give you absolute control. Few dogs can bolt from you when held in this manner.

Draw a line with a pen on the middle portion of the leash where it loops over your thumb. This will help you find the right location each time you use the leash. Draw a second line on the sewn loop at the top of the leash to remind you to hook it onto your thumb.

The Corrective Jerk

The corrective jerk is used extensively throughout this course and is an integral part of it. This important teaching tool sends a signal to the dog in the most effective, direct manner that he did the wrong thing. The leash and training collar represent a line of communication that sends corrective signals to the dog. Using them properly is a significant aspect of obedience training and solving dog problems. However, the corrective jerk must only be used as a means of communication and not as a form of punishment. *Please note that young puppies should not wear training collars. They should be corrected gently with a leash and buckled collar.*

The corrective jerk is a correction involving a quick, gentle tug of the leash that tightens the training collar around the dog's neck for an instant. It sends an unmistakable, negative signal. If the trainer jerks the leash too hard, it is abusive and ineffective. If the trainer jerks the leash too softly, it communicates nothing to the dog. Administering the correction properly depends on the personality and temperament of the dog being taught. The point is to communicate a negative message; nothing more, nothing less.

Administering the Corrective Jerk

Stand to the right of the dog, facing in the same direction. Hold the leash as described above. Quickly jerk it to your right side in a horizontal direction. When jerking the leash, do it firmly, releasing the tension on the leash *immediately* following the jerk by returning your arms quickly to their original position. *This is very important.* Do not jerk the leash forward or in any direction other than to your right side.

The dog will feel the correction as the training collar tightens for an instant around his neck. It gives him an unmistakable signal that he performed incorrectly or that he did not listen to you. As you administer each leash correction, say, "NO," in a firm tone of voice and then follow it with verbal praise. *It is essential that you praise the dog immediately following each correction.*

The correction communicates to the dog that he did the wrong thing, and the praise reassures him that he is still accepted and loved as a member of the family. The praise is also given as a reward for accepting the correction. Your dog will work for your praise as his reward. Corrections and rewards reinforce the teaching process and effectively motivate the dog.

Do not practice leash corrections on your dog. They will confuse and upset him. All corrections must serve a purpose and be given for incorrect performance or misbehavior. Corrections must be fair.

"NO" and "OKAY"

"NO" is a verbal correction, and is an important training tool. When you correct a dog, it is important to say, "NO," with a firm, resonant sound in order to get the dog's attention and convince him that you mean business. The verbal correction is simply one word, "NO," but must never be hollered out in anger. When the correction "NO" is said properly, the dog should stop whatever he is doing instantly and totally accept your authority.

The corrective jerk must always be accompanied with the verbal correction "NO." However, the verbal correction "NO" does not always require the corrective jerk. Eventually, "NO," stated firmly, will suffice without the need for any other correction.

"OKAY" is a positive-sounding command that gets a dog to anticipate forward movement or a release from discipline. Use it as a positive tag to your dog's name when giving him a command involving forward motion such as "HEEL" or "COME." Example: "OKAY, Jason, HEEL!" It must always sound upbeat and happy.

"OKAY" is the ideal command for telling your dog that he is released from his training session or from a formal walk. After walking in HEEL you may want to release your dog so that he can relieve himself. Simply say, "OKAY," and allow him to use the full length of the leash to get to the curb. "OKAY" should always be said in a happy, enthusiastic tone of voice with the emphasis on the *O*. Releasing your dog from a training session with this command should inspire the dog to prance with pleasure.

Leash Breaking

You cannot obedience-train a dog unless he is wearing a leash and collar. Leash breaking should begin soon after you bring your young dog home. Goldens usually have no difficulty adjusting to the leash but like all puppies may resist wearing it for the first time because they do not want their movements to be restrained. The reaction to wearing a leash for the first time varies in puppies from immediate acceptance to stubborn refusal to fear. Some puppies bite the leash and try to pull it off with their paws.

Get your new dog to accept his leash by placing a buckled collar around his neck with a lightweight leash attached to it. Let him drag it around all day for several days. (*Never leave your dog, young or old, alone with a leash attached to his collar. Doing so could lead to a fatal accident.*)

The dog will probably adjust to wearing the leash and collar in one to three days. Be certain the buckled collar is comfortable. Always be cheerful and upbeat when attaching the leash to the collar. Create a pleasant association with it. Offer a food tidbit as you do this.

Entice the puppy to follow you and walk around the house while dragging the leash. After a while, pick up the leash and walk around with the dog. Stay relaxed and upbeat as though you were taking a casual stroll. As you hold the leash, entice the dog to walk with you in a playful manner allowing as much slack as possible. Do this as often as possible for the entire leash breaking period.

Once the dog has made an adjustment to the leash by wearing it around the house, especially with you holding it, try walking him outdoors. It is preferable to start out on a soft, grassy surface. If he resists walking with the leash, the grass will prevent his paws from being painfully scraped as they would be on a hard, rough sidewalk.

If your puppy refuses to walk while attached to the leash, drop to your knees and call him to you in a very happy, cheerful tone of voice. Do not drag him, holler at him, or punish him in any way. Make him feel safe and loved. Try to create a pleasant association with the leash. When the little dog finally comes to you, praise him lavishly, stand up, and start to walk with him as you hold the leash with as much slack as possible.

It is common for a puppy to paw or bite the leash when having it placed around his neck for the first time. When that happens, give the dog a verbal correction. Say, "NO," in a mild but firm tone of

1. As you say the command "S-I-I-I-T," hold the leash taut with your right hand and gently but firmly pull the leash upward. 2. At the same time, gently but firmly push the dog's rear end downward with your left hand.

voice and pull the leash away from him. It is essential to praise the dog enthusiastically immediately after each correction.

About the Command "SIT"

When given the command "SIT," your dog is expected to sit erect on his haunches. He must move into an upright position with his front legs straight and vertically extended in front of his body. The dog's attention should be fixed on his trainer.

Teaching SIT requires a training collar and a six-foot leather leash for an adolescent or adult dog. Young puppies should wear a buckle-type collar. Attach the leash to the collar and hold it with your right hand as previously instructed in The Corrective Jerk (page 107).

Work with a shortened leash by gathering up the slack in your right hand, allowing approximately one foot of it to remain between the collar and your left hand. With only a short length of leash available to the dog, you will have all the control necessary for teaching the command.

Teaching SIT to a high-energy Golden is difficult in the beginning because he will be fidgety and excitable. You have the option of training your dog indoors or outdoors, depending on his energy level. Select a quiet outdoor area with no one present or a small, quiet area of your home, such as a hallway. If indoors, place your dog against a wall so he cannot move to the left and out of your reach. Handle him with short-leash control, no more than one or two feet of leash.

You may teach SIT to a Golden of moderate temperament indoors or outdoors with no spectators present. Moderate-tempered dogs require a very gentle, light touch. Be patient and calm, using mild corrections when necessary. Praise should be given with exuberance to a moderate-tempered dog. You may hug him and do anything that builds his confidence. Train him in a quiet place with no distractions. If the dog is fearful and lowers his head in submissiveness, try using motivational aids, such as food treats, a ball, or even a squeaky toy.

The idea is to get the dog to look up at you as you teach the command. Praise, love, and affection are the most important tools for dogs of this temperament.

Teaching SIT

1. Start out on your dog's right side, facing in the same direction. Stand next to a high-energy dog or kneel on one knee next to a moderate-tempered dog. Hold approximately one foot of the leash taut over the dog's head with your right hand.

2. Hold the dog at the base of his spine (at the hip joints) with your left hand. You will feel two indentations. With a firm grip, press them gently with your fingers.

3. Say the command "S-I-I-I-T," stretching the word out as you say it. It is best to use a cheerful tone of voice that descends in tone as the dog moves down into position.

4. As you say the command, push the dog's rear end downward with your left hand as you pull the front of his body gently upward by the leash with your right hand.

Puppies and adult dogs alike learn this command easily and quickly and can be maneuvered into the proper position without difficulty. Once your dog is in SIT, tell him how smart he is, even though you placed him in the proper position. With repetition of the teaching steps, the dog will quickly learn SIT on command.

A high-energy dog may nip at you or mouth your hands or legs as you try to teach him this command. When he does, give him a quick leash correction and a firm "NO" the instant he misbehaves. Repeat the command "SIT" and then praise him. The praise should be moderate, because the more expressive you are with him the more he is going to want to stop and play.

Once the dog understands what is expected of him, try giving the command without pushing him in place. Say, "SIT," and gently raise the leash with your right hand. Praise him each time he goes into the SIT position.

Next, eliminate pulling up the leash. Say, "SIT," and do not apply any hand or leash pressure. Praise the dog each time he obeys the command properly.

Try giving the command in different parts of the house and get him to obey without squirming around. Next, take the dog outdoors and give him the command. Once he performs properly outdoors, give him the command with more and more slack in the leash. The result should be that you can give the command "SIT" from six feet away from the dog, from the front of him, the side of him, the back of him. When he can respond in all those situations, you can expose him to other animals as you give him the command.

As your dog becomes tired, end the session on a high note after the successful completion of the command. Allow the dog to have a bowl of water, to relieve himself, and to take a nap.

About the Command "SIT-STAY"

When given the command "STAY," your dog is expected to remain in the SIT position until released from the command. The dog's attention should be fixed on his trainer.

STAY is a difficult command for high-energy Golden Retrievers. They are fidgety dogs, constantly moving and looking around and eager to play. The command may be taught indoors or outdoors, depending on the energy level of your dog. Teach STAY in a quiet area, with no spectators present. If you train indoors, select a hallway to work in. That will enable you to box in a highly energetic dog with the wall at his back and a barrier on his left and right side. He'll have no choice but to remain in the SIT position without moving in any direction. Chairs on each side of the dog will serve as barriers. Whether working indoors or outdoors, in the beginning, a quiet environment is important if the dog is expected to concentrate on what you teach him.

As you teach the dog, repeat the verbal commands often if your Golden is a high-energy type. Correct him with a firm but not harsh

1. Start by giving the command "SIT." The dog should be sitting on your left side looking at you attentively.

2. After giving the command "STAY," place your left hand four inches away from the dog's eyes.

3. After the "pivotal turn" and the command "STAY," stand in front of the dog until you release him from the command.

4. Repeat all the steps as you teach the dog SIT-STAY from one, two, three, and six feet away.

tone of voice. When you praise the dog, do not be too high-spirited or he will become excited and playful.

Moderate-tempered Goldens have a much easier time with STAY because they will remain in one place, but for the wrong reason—insecurity. Use an open space, indoors, without barriers on the sides of the dog when teaching the command. Insecure dogs should be encouraged to be somewhat playful and outgoing. Praise dogs of this type with energy, exuberance, and an excited, high-pitched voice as if talking to a baby. Try whining like a puppy. Get the dog to enjoy the session by getting his attention and keeping it.

During teaching techniques involving side-to-side movements as the dog stays in place, use quick motions with a bounce to your step as you walk around him. Keep talking as you maneuver through the teaching process, repeating the command and congratulating the dog for staying in place. Never allow a moderate-tempered dog to become bored or uninterested.

Teaching SIT-STAY

The instructions for STAY involve a verbal command, a hand signal, and a special pivotal turn on the ball of your left foot.

1. With the dog on your left side, stand side by side, facing the same direction. Hold the leash in your right hand, with two or three feet draped across your knees. Give the command "SIT." If the dog does not obey, give him a leash correction at the same time, saying, "NO," in a firm but not harsh tone of voice. Praise the dog for the sake of reassurance. He should go into the proper position. Praise him again. If he does not, go back to teaching SIT.

2. Say the command "STAY," and use the hand signal. The hand signal is given with the left hand as you hold the leash with your right hand. Flatten your left hand as if for a salute and place it in front of the dog's face with your palm facing his eyes. As you give the command "STAY," place your left hand four inches away from the front of his eyes. Do not touch the dog's eyes. The dog's vision should be

blocked only for an instant. Place your left hand under your right hand, on the leash. Eventually, the dog will remain in STAY with the use of the hand signal alone.

3. With both hands on the leash, make a pivotal turn on your left foot so that you end up facing the dog as he remains in the SIT-STAY position. To do this, swivel on the ball of your left foot as you slowly move the right foot in front of the dog. As the right foot moves in place, your body will turn with it. Slide your left foot over to your right so that they are slightly apart. You should now be facing the dog. Throughout the pivotal turn you must keep holding the leash above his head to keep him in position. If you do this any other way, the dog will assume you are about to move forward and start to go with you.

The leash must be taut and held upward, to the side of the dog, so that it does not hit him on the chin. Leash control is the most important teaching element in this command. In a subdued tone of voice congratulate the dog for not moving (despite the fact that you held him in place with the leash). Repeat this step several times, keeping the dog in the STAY position for thirty seconds each time. Praise him for his accurate responses and correct him for his errors. The pivotal turn is merely a teaching tool and will not be used after the dog has learned the command thoroughly.

4. The next step is to teach the dog to remain in SIT-STAY as you stand in front of him from a distance of one, two, three, and six feet, until he is released from the command. This is a gradual process requiring diligence from the trainer as well as the dog.

From one foot away. Repeat steps 1, 2, and 3 until you are certain the dog will remain sitting in front of you while you are one foot away from him.

5. *From two feet away.* While still holding the leash above the dog's head, transfer it to the left hand, placing the thumb inside the loop at the very top. With the right hand, grasp the leash eighteen inches above the collar and hold it loosely. The leash must be able to slide through the right hand once you start to move away from the dog.

The technique will eliminate any slack from developing as you move away. If the leash slackens, you will be unable to force the dog to remain in SIT-STAY.

While standing in front of the dog, back away approximately two feet, allowing the leash to extend but always in a taut position. The dog may try to move toward you. Say, "NO," as you quickly return to your original position by the dog's right side, praise him, and maintain a taut leash extended above the dog's head. Stand next to the dog once again and repeat steps 1, 2, and 3. Wait thirty seconds and try backing away again. Repeat this procedure until the dog finally holds his position from two feet away, for which you must praise him. Repeat the process until you feel the dog has learned the command at that distance.

6. *From three feet away*. Repeat steps 1, 2, and 3. As you back away from the dog, allow the leash to slide through your right hand as you hold it with the loop around the thumb of your left hand. As you move backward, keep the leash taut, allowing it to extend between you and the dog. Do not pull on the leash or the dog will walk toward you. If he does, repeat the command "STAY" in a firm tone of voice and move in toward him, back to a distance of one foot. As you move forward, pull the leash through your right hand with your left hand and then hold it above his head as much as possible. In most instances the dog will stop moving as you take your first step toward him. If he does, praise him. Begin backing away again after several seconds, until you reach your goal of three feet in front of the dog. Praise him. Hold the position for thirty seconds. Repeat the process until you feel the dog has learned the command at that distance.

7. *From six feet away*. Do not attempt SIT-STAY from six feet until you are certain the dog can remain in position from the shorter distances. Always start out the session with the shorter distances. With that accomplished, proceed to six feet.

Repeat steps 1, 2, and 3. As before, slowly walk backward one step at a time. Command the dog, "STAY," and praise him after each step. Use a firm but gentle tone of voice that is soft and soothing. Your tone of voice is important so as not to entice the dog to move toward you. Bear in mind that you no longer have the same level of leash control at this distance. As you back away, the dog is quite likely to run to you. If that happens, give him the command "STAY," and step forward to block him, shortening the leash quickly by sliding it through your right hand as you pull it with your left hand. Hold it taut above his head. Give him the command "SIT." As he obeys, praise him, wait a few seconds, and back slowly away until you reach the full extent of the six-foot leash. Remain standing in front of him for thirty seconds so he absorbs the meaning of STAY. Return to your original position and repeat all the steps until you are satisfied that the dog has successfully learned to obey the command from six feet.

8. *Walking around the dog.* You are now ready to teach your dog to hold the position as you walk around each side of him and then walk around him in a complete circle.

Repeat steps 1, 2, and 3. Walk halfway around the dog's right side from two feet in front of him. Remember to hold the leash taut above his head. Return quickly to the front position. Do it several times. Once he tolerates that movement without leaving his position, try walking around to his left side and returning. With that accomplished, walk a complete circle around the dog as he holds his STAY position. As you succeed in these motions, increase the distance as in the earlier steps until you can walk completely around the dog from six feet away.

Once the dog obeys sufficiently to hold his position as you walk around him from six feet, move in front of him and turn your back to him. Your dog has completely mastered the command "SIT-STAY" when you can command him to "SIT" and then "STAY."

End each training session on a happy note of success.

About the Command "HEEL" *and the Automatic* SIT

HEEL

HEEL means your dog must walk with you on command, paying attention so that he keeps pace with you, turns with you, and never pulls ahead or lags behind. The dog must stay on your left side, keeping his head even with your left leg, and stop when you stop.

A high-energy Golden is going to be distracted by anything and everything when you try to teach him the command "HEEL." As you start out, the dog will run to the end of the leash, pulling with excitement. He will run in all directions, bouncing to the left, bouncing to the right, jumping all over the place. To bring your dog under control, train him in a quiet area where there are no distractions or spectators. Once the dog has mastered the command, you may practice in a busy area to test his ability to obey.

When rewarding a high-energy dog with verbal praise for obeying properly, do not be too exuberant. Modify your tone of voice so that he doesn't become excited and jump all over you, making it impossible to go on with the lesson. Give him just enough encouragement to perform properly and want to be with you. You may lavish praise on him at the end of each training session.

The moderate-tempered Golden, whether he is shy, unsure of himself, reserved, or simply hesitant, will probably walk behind you in the beginning. He may cling to you or trot hesitantly by your side. Sensitive dogs such as these should be given mild leash corrections, and not too many of them. These dogs should also be trained in a quiet area with no distractions or spectators. Once the dog has mastered the command, you may practice in a busy area to test his ability to obey.

When praising moderate-tempered dogs, use a high-pitched tone of voice that is playful and friendly. Every time you pause during the teaching sessions, kneel down to the dog's level and praise him affectionately. If you constantly stand over the dog, towering above him,

1. Begin teaching the command "HEEL" by placing the dog at the your left side, giving him the command "SIT" and then "STAY," using the appropriate hand signal. Praise him if he obeys properly.

2. The command "HEEL" requires using the dog's name first. Say, "George, HEEL," and step forward with your left foot.

you will cultivate a submissive personality. Encourage him with hugs, kisses, and praise to give him confidence in you and in himself. Unlike the high-energy dog, he can even be allowed to jump on you in order to make him more outgoing.

Be very physical in your movements when teaching this command. Make quick and sudden turns, changing your pace frequently, walking slowly one minute and fast the next. Try to motivate moderate-tempered dogs and get them to walk close to you. Try using squeak toys, balls, or even food treats if that's what it takes to bring the dog out of his shell. The more you express loving playfulness the quicker the dog will learn to walk in HEEL.

Limit each training session to fifteen minutes and conduct no more than two a day, spaced at least four hours apart. However, you may practice walking in HEEL many times during the day, especially if you have an errand to run. Practice walking in HEEL when you take your dog out to relieve himself. The more you practice, the sooner the dog will master the command.

Teaching the Command "HEEL"

High-energy dogs require firm corrections and subdued praise. Moderate-tempered Goldens require mild corrections, playful coaxing, and energized praise.

1. With the dog at your left side, attach the training collar and six-foot leather leash, as described earlier. Both arms should dangle at your sides in a relaxed position. Hold the leash at the halfway mark with your right hand and allow the remaining half to drape across your knees, hooked onto the dog's collar.

2. Give your dog the command "SIT," and praise him if he obeys. Next, give the command "STAY," using the appropriate hand signal. Hold the leash in your right hand in the normal manner, ready to correct the dog if necessary. Once again, praise him if he obeys properly.

3. In the verbal command for HEEL, the dog's name is said first, followed by the word "HEEL." "HEEL" is a forward-motion command, and the dog's name is what gets his attention, along with the movement of your left foot. "HEEL" is a command that propels your dog into forward motion. His name is actually a signal getting him ready to move forward.

Say, "George, HEEL." As you say the word "HEEL," step forward with your left foot. It is closest to the dog's line of sight and will get him moving the instant you step off. The first thing your high-energy dog will do is run ahead of you.

4. Just before the dog reaches the end of the leash, make a very firm right U-turn and stride in the opposite direction. This may take a great deal of strength, depending on the dog. As you begin your turn, say, "George, HEEL," in a loud, firm tone of voice. The dog will be stopped suddenly from running ahead and forced to move quickly to catch up with you. In effect, he will have corrected himself. Keep walking briskly in the opposite direction. This turn of events comes as an abrupt surprise to the dog. He has no choice but to keep up with you or feel the force of the leash pulling him in your direction. In the most definite sense this action establishes you in the dominant, yet loving, position. It is the first time that you really begin to gain control over the dog. You will be imposing your will over his impulsive desires.

5. As the dog tries to catch up with you, tap your left leg in a friendly manner and invite him to get closer. Try get him to position his head next to your leg. Praise him as he gets near you.

6. If your dog runs past you again, repeat the right U-turn procedure and keep repeating it until the dog learns to keep pace with you and maintain the proper position. With each repetition the dog will walk closer and closer to you, and eventually will walk with you, in the proper position, keeping his head next to your left leg.

Whenever the dog fails to maintain the correct HEEL position, administer a leash correction. Gently jerk the leash to your right and say, "George, HEEL," execute a U-turn, and walk in the opposite direction. Praise a high-energy dog in a subdued manner and a moderate-tempered dog with enthusiasm and exuberance.

Shy, sensitive Goldens tend to lag behind or go off to the left or cling to your legs. Do not give your dog too many leash corrections. Rely more on enticement with your voice and friendly body language. Walk slowly, change your pace, run, walk faster, make many quick turns. Sensitive Goldens are not going to want to be at the end of the leash and must be motivated to keep up. Balls, squeak toys, gentle tugs of the leash, and even food tidbits are desirable motivators. The trick is to get the dog to walk close to you without a lot of leash corrections.

Talking to your sensitive dog or young puppy is the best answer. Playfully encourage him to catch up and keep pace. The happy sound of your voice can make all the difference.

If necessary, kneel and call the dog to you. When he reaches you, rise quickly and begin walking in the same direction. If the dog or puppy does not respond properly, you may gently snap the leash with a slight jerk or pull. What is desirable is to keep the dog focused on you.

Automatic SIT

Every time the dog walks in HEEL he must stop when you stop and SIT without being given a command. After being given the command "STAY" (and then being praised), he must hold his position until he is released or given the next command, which is usually "HEEL."

This command is accomplished by communicating to the dog that you are going to stop walking. You simply slow down before coming to a halt. Slowing down as you walk is a signal to the dog to be ready to stop and SIT, automatically, once you stop moving forward. This is one of the reasons it is important for the dog to stay focused on you when walking in HEEL.

Teaching Automatic SIT

1. Begin the lesson by placing the dog in the SIT-STAY position.

2. Give the command, "Jason, HEEL" (praise the dog immediately after giving the command), and walk in HEEL for at least one minute at a moderate speed. Gradually slow down until you finally stop walking.

3. Give the dog the command "SIT." If he obeys, as he should by now, reward him with praise. Remember, high-energy dogs must be given praise in a subdued tone of voice, while moderate-tempered dogs must be praised with exuberance.

4. If the dog does not respond properly to the command, say, "NO," in a firm tone of voice and administer a corrective jerk by tugging the leash upward and to the right side, immediately following up

with praise. If he was taught SIT properly, the dog should obey the command after the correction. If he still does not respond properly, say, "SIT," and follow up with another leash correction to reinforce the command. If the dog does not respond to this, you must return to Teaching SIT, page 113, and teach the command all over again. Once the dog obeys the command and places himself in the SIT position on command, praise him in the appropriate manner.

5. Getting the dog to sit automatically after walking in HEEL is the result of repeating the above procedures for at least twenty minutes, several times a day. Give the dog a break after each ten minutes of repetition and finish the lesson after the next ten minutes. End the session by saying, "OKAY," in a happy tone of voice, allow the dog to relieve himself, and then happily walk home.

6. Practice this command every day until the dog sits automatically after walking in HEEL without being commanded to do it.

About the Commands "DOWN" *and* "DOWN-STAY"

DOWN

The command "DOWN" is given verbally and with a hand signal. On command, the dog must lower himself to the ground, where he remains with his head erect and his front legs extended forward. He may lower his head and place his chin on the ground if he must remain in position for more than a few minutes.

This is the most difficult command for any dog to learn and accept. DOWN is the ultimate position of subordination. It also demands of the dog that he obey the command and control his instinct to react impulsively to anything that stimulates him. For these reasons it is important to begin the training of high-energy or moderate-tempered Goldens in a quiet, indoor area with no one else present and with as few distractions as possible.

Because the dog's front legs initially must be slid into position when being taught this command, the surface of the floor is an important consideration. The best surface is linoleum because of its smoothness. Other surfaces, especially carpet, create friction, which could be painful when sliding the dog into the DOWN position. A smooth surface also allows the command to be taught with far less effort.

Two teaching techniques are offered here for the first part of this command. The first one, the *push-and-pull technique,* is suited for high-energy Goldens. The second one, the *sweep technique,* is best for moderate-tempered Goldens. After teaching either one of these techniques, you must go on to teach the remaining aspects of the command, which involve the hand technique and the front technique.

The verbal command

When saying the command word "DOWN," extend the middle portion of the word so that it is spoken in a longer, exaggerated way. The sound you make should start at a high point and get lower and lower as you reach the end of the word: "DOWWwwnnnn." It is like music to a dancer and will help the dog move properly to the sound of your voice. As your voice descends in tone, it should inspire your dog to do the same with his body.

The hand signal

This important aspect of the command is taught when the dog is placed in the DOWN position by applying pressure on the extended training collar with your hand. This part of the teaching occurs in the hand technique and the front technique.

The hand signal requires that you flatten your left hand as if for a military salute as you face the dog. Raise your left arm fully above your head. Say the command "DOWWwwnnnn," and lower the left arm at a steady rate of movement so that the dog sees it coming down. The objective is to associate your lowering arm with the command "DOWN." Once this is accomplished, you will be able to stand a good distance from the dog and simply give him the hand signal, to which he will respond as he should. Praise him after each command and signal is given.

Say, "DOWWwwnnnn," and lower your left arm past the dog's eyes and onto the top of the leash.

Teaching DOWN with the Push-and-Pull Technique
(for High-Energy Goldens)

1. Place the dog on your left side with both of you facing in the same direction. Hold the leash properly with both hands and do not allow any slack in it. (See Holding the Leash Properly, page 107.) Say, "SIT," and praise the dog for obeying. Say, "STAY," using the hand signal described in Teaching SIT-STAY, page 116. Praise the dog again.

2. Kneel next to the dog's right side and place the leash in your left hand. You will have better control of the dog if you take up all the slack in the leash so that you can hold him in position if necessary.

3. Place your left hand (with the leash in it) on the dog's shoulder, just above the neck, gripping it with your thumb and middle finger. Take hold of the dog's right front leg just above the paw.

4. Say the command "DOWWwwnnnn," and push the dog's shoulder downward with your left hand as you lift his right leg, pulling it forward and slightly out to the right side. These combined actions get the dog into a DOWN position on the ground. If the dog tends to favor his left leg as he stands, then pull his left leg out instead. Keep the leash as taut as possible as the dog moves downward. Praise him for going into the DOWN position, even though you placed him there.

5. Once the dog is DOWN you may hold him in that position for ten seconds by placing your foot on the leash. Otherwise, he will jump out of position instantly.

6. Repeat this procedure ten or fifteen times, until the dog offers little or no resistance to being placed in DOWN. Some dogs go into the proper position on command without being placed there at this stage of the teaching. Most do not. You may end the session here and practice these steps several times a day until the next lesson.

You are now ready to continue on to the next step, which is the hand technique, skipping the following sweep technique for moderate-tempered Goldens.

It is important to understand that this technique is only the first step when teaching DOWN. After teaching the push-and-pull technique you must continue with the hand technique and the front technique. These are essential.

Teaching DOWN with the Sweep Technique (for Moderate-Tempered Goldens)

1. Place the dog on your left side with both of you facing in the same direction. Hold the leash properly with both hands and do not allow any slack in it. (See Holding The Leash Properly, page 107.) Say, "SIT," and praise the dog for obeying. Say, "STAY," using the hand signal described in Teaching SIT-STAY, page 116. Praise the dog again.

2. Kneel next to the dog's right side and place the leash in your left hand. You will have better control of the dog if you take up all

the slack in the leash so that you can hold him in position if necessary.

3. Place your right hand behind the dog's front legs, near his
belly.

4. In a firm voice say, "DOWWwwnnnn," in the exaggerated
manner recommended for the verbal command, page 126. Given the
sensitive nature of moderate-tempered Goldens, your voice should
be gentle, soothing, firm but loving.

5. As you say the command "DOWWwwnnnn," glide your right
hand under the dog's belly toward the chest, moving his legs upward
and to the front so that he must gently go into the DOWN position.
As the dog's legs move off the ground, keep your right hand in motion until he is in the DOWN position. Praise your dog each time
you do this.

6. Repeat these steps ten or fifteen times or until the dog offers no
resistance to being placed in the DOWN position. He may begin to
go into DOWN without being placed in position by the end of this
teaching step. You may end the session here and practice several
times a day until the next training lesson.

You are now ready to continue on to the next step, the hand technique.

Teaching DOWN with the Hand Technique
(for High-Energy and Moderate-Tempered Goldens)

*Whether you used the push-and-pull technique or the sweep technique to ma-
neuver the dog into the DOWN position, you must now add the use of your
hand as part of the teaching process. This phase of the command is necessary
for teaching the dog to respond to the hand signal without a command.*

1. Place the dog on your left side with both of you facing in the
same direction. Hold the leash properly with both hands and do not
allow any slack in it. Say, "SIT," and praise the dog for obeying. Say,
"STAY," using the hand signal described in Teaching SIT-STAY,
page 116. Praise the dog again.

2. Kneel next to the dog's right side. Hold the leash with the right

hand across your chest and keep it taut. With a tight leash he can do nothing but SIT. Flatten your left hand as if for a military salute. Raise your left arm above your head.

3. Say the command "DOWWwwnnnn," and lower the left arm so that the dog can see it coming down past his eyes and onto the top of the taut leash where the clip attaches to the training collar. By now the dog should be lowering his body in response to the verbal command.

4. While you are still saying "DOWWwwnnnn," your left hand should be pressing the leash all the way to the ground. Praise the dog as he reaches the ground.

5. Repeat this procedure at least fifteen times. The objective is for the dog to associate your lowering hand with the command "DOWN." With this accomplished, you will eventually be able to give the hand signal alone for DOWN from a good distance away and get him to obey the command. If the dog does not respond properly or resists the teaching of this part of the lesson, place him in SIT-STAY and begin again. You may end the session here, but you must practice this technique several times a day until the next training lesson.

Teaching DOWN with the Front Technique
(for High-Energy and Moderate-Tempered Goldens)

The front technique is the next logical step for teaching DOWN. This step familiarizes the dog with the hand signal as it will be used in the future and indoctrinates him in responding to it properly.

Now that the dog has learned to be pushed into DOWN with your hand on the leash from the side, it is safe to assume that you can accomplish the same thing from the front. Your dog's proper response to the hand signal is an important step in reinforcing his understanding of the entire command.

1. Hold the leash properly in your right hand and place the dog in SIT-STAY using the appropriate hand signal.

2. Pivot around on the ball of your left foot so that you stand directly in front of the dog, about two feet away from him. Switch the

leash to your left hand. Hold it taut and as high above the dog's head as possible without bending your body forward.

3. Raise your right hand as high as you can with your fingers extended straight and close to each other.

4. Say, "DOWWwwnnnn." As you give the command, lower your right hand in a steady, deliberate manner onto the leash. Push the top of the leash hard with your right hand, pressing it downward toward the ground. This teaches the dog to associate your lowering hand signal with the "DOWN" command and to comply with it. Elongate the verbal command "DOWWwwnnnn" until the dog is actually in the proper DOWN position.

5. If your dog lowers himself into DOWN without being pushed into position with the pressure of your descending hand, praise him enthusiastically and then repeat the exercise fifteen times. It is important to praise the dog the instant he is all the way down each time. Remember, the dog works for the praise. It is his motivation to please you. This is an appropriate place to end the session. Practice this step several times a day until the next training lesson.

The very next stage is to teach the front technique from greater distances. Simply repeat all five steps of the front technique in the following sessions but move farther away from the dog each time. Repeat the five steps from three feet away. After the dog succeeds from three feet, move to four feet, and so on, until he will obey from the fully extended leash, or six feet. If you are ambitious, you may tie a long clothesline to the end of the leash and continually train the dog from even greater distances.

Once the dog responds properly from greater distances, the next phase is to repeat the front technique but without pushing or even touching the leash with your hand as you lower your arm. Allow your hand to brush past the leash without actually touching it. This will be exactly the way your hand signal will look from a distance. Repeat this phase until the dog obeys the command "DOWN" perfectly from your verbal command only and then from hand signal only.

The teaching technique for DOWN-STAY is similar to that for SIT-STAY except that the dog is placed in a down position. The hand signal for STAY is an essential aspect of this command.

Teaching DOWN-STAY

To teach DOWN-STAY, return to the SIT-STAY lesson in this chapter and follow it completely. The only difference is to place the dog in DOWN wherever it instructs you to place the dog in SIT.

DOWN-STAY means your dog remains in the DOWN position on the ground or on the floor until you release him from the command. It is similar to SIT-STAY except that the dog goes into a DOWN position. The teaching techniques are identical to those of SIT-STAY. If the dog now responds properly to SIT-STAY, it can be assumed that he will have no difficulty learning DOWN-STAY. STAY in the DOWN position may confuse some dogs and they will require further teaching of the command, but it will be more of a refresher course. In that instance, repeat the teaching steps of SIT-STAY until the dog responds properly. Then continue on to DOWN-STAY using the same teaching techniques.

About the Command

"COME WHEN CALLED"

On command, your dog must instantly stop whatever he is doing and come running to you quickly. When he arrives at your feet, he must go into a SIT position. The sequence involves a verbal command and a hand signal.

The foundation for this command is your dog's anticipation of pleasure when answering your call. A young Golden Retriever should fly to you with delight when you call him, providing that you have never scolded him when he got to you. If you have always clapped your hands happily and praised your dog when he came to you since the day you brought him home, then teaching this command will be much easier. Why would a dog (or a person) run to anyone only to be hollered at, hit, or disciplined?

It is not too late to create this feeling in your dog if you hug him and tell him how wonderful he is after you call him. Always be enthusiastic when he gets to you, and give him a lot of praise. The best possibility for teaching this command successfully is to make coming to you a very pleasant event.

The High-Energy Golden

Teaching COME WHEN CALLED to this type of Golden can be great fun, considering the joyful enthusiasm of the breed. The problem, however, is how his energy level affects his responses to you. Some dogs are easily distracted and will promptly lose their focus and concentration. Another problem is calling the untrained dog to you. He will make a mad dash in your general direction, zigzagging along the way, and end up crashing into your legs. Sometimes it is funny and sometimes it is painful.

At the start, teach COME WHEN CALLED in a quiet, indoor environment, with no distractions and no audience. You may move the lessons to a closed-in outdoor area with some distractions once the dog has learned the basics of the command and responds appropriately to them.

At the start of this command, use only two feet of the six-foot leash. It will give you more control over the dog while teaching the command. The more control you have when teaching the command, the quicker the dog will learn. A Golden will always come to you when you call him. However, a well-trained Golden will come straight to you and sit properly in front of you wherever you are standing. Critical leash control will accomplish that.

The training environment should be indoors, in a long hallway, so the dog will learn from the beginning to move toward you in a straight line. Set up a chute so the dog cannot veer to the left or right but must move straight to you when you call him. You can improvise a chute with anything: a wall and several chairs, two long benches, long planks of wood, a dog-run, etcetera. An improvised chute will get a high-energy dog to focus on moving directly to you as you teach the command. Don't forget to praise the dog when he reaches you.

When praising the dog, use a moderate tone of voice that is not too high in pitch; otherwise he will become excited. The most important elements are firm leash control and knowing where exactly you want the dog to be when he gets to you.

As you call the dog, move backward quickly so you can make adjustments with the leash and training collar and guide the dog into a straight line directly in front of you. The secret to teaching this command is positioning the dog properly as he comes to you.

An important aspect of this command is teaching the dog to go into a SIT position once he reaches you. In the beginning, however, do not worry about a high-energy Golden sitting properly as he gets to you. It is more important that he come to you on command. If you are too critical, you may discourage him from responding to your call. The first part of the command is getting the dog to come to you, and the second part is getting him to SIT properly.

The Moderate-Tempered Golden

A more reserved, sensitive type of Golden must be motivated to come to you on command. Use a fifteen- or thirty-foot leash (clothesline will do) so that the dog has a longer distance to get to you as you move backward. He may resist a six-foot leash when it is pulled. During the teaching process, try moving backward quickly as the dog comes toward you. This may energize the dog or at least appeal to his playfulness. Use a high-pitched tone of voice oozing with exuberance. Motivational aids such as balls, squeak toys, whistles, or any attention-getters are useful if they can get the dog to come to you without fear or hesitation.

Sometimes you can get a dog of this type to run to you by arousing his curiosity with distractions that are just behind you, such as a toy, another dog, or even another person.

Always keep the dog on-leash as you work outdoors, in a safe, fenced-off area, just in case he bolts and you lose control of him. Do not teach this command outdoors if the dog is off-leash. Off-leash training is not part of this course and can be hazardous if not taught correctly.

Throughout the life of your moderate-tempered Golden, it is important that he associate your call with a happy experience. If you call him and then correct him, he will stop coming to you. Never call your dog to correct his misbehavior. If you need to correct him, always go to him.

Teaching COME WHEN CALLED

The verbal command

COME WHEN CALLED requires three words, "OKAY, Solly, COME." Each of the three words is a separate part of the command.

Draw out the *ohhh*, when you say, "*OHHH*-KAY," and place the accent on the *Oh*. Raise the pitch of your voice so it sounds cheerful. The word "OKAY" will create a feeling of pleasant anticipation in your dog if it is said in a happy, upbeat tone.

1. Place your dog in SIT and SIT-STAY and step back. 2. Give him the verbal command, "OKAY, Solly, COME." Swing your extended right arm around to your chest and gently tug the leash. The dog should walk toward you. 3. Your dog should SIT and STAY as he reaches you.

The dog's name is meant to prepare him for forward motion. Let your voice rise and say the name cheerfully.

"COME" is the actual command word. It tells him exactly what you want him to do and therefore must be said with conviction and emphasis.

Call your dog in the same way every time: "*O*KAY, Solly, COME!" Always give the command for COME WHEN CALLED in this precise manner and have the other members of your family do the same.

The hand signal

The verbal command is always given with a hand signal. It eliminates confusion when calling the dog from a distance. The right arm leaves the side of the body and is raised, swinging to the left, toward the left shoulder. It is the same gesture used to call someone to you.

1. Repeat all the commands the dog has learned up to this point.

2. Place your dog in a SIT-STAY position. With only two feet of slack, hold the leash in your left hand and step in front of the dog, facing him.

3. Say, "OKAY, Solly, COME."

4. Do two things as you say, "OKAY." Motion the dog to come to you by quickly swinging your extended right arm around to your chest and gently tug on the leash with your left hand. Finish the command, "Solly, COME." You have just given the verbal command and the hand signal.

5. The dog should move forward as you say the command and tug the leash. As soon as you have given the hand signal, place your right hand on the leash, using it with the left hand in a hand-over-hand motion to reel the leash in like a fishing line. As the dog reaches you, the leash should be gathered in your hands. Praise the dog for coming to you.

6. Repeat these five steps at least fifteen times. If he does not move toward you, then add more excitement to the tone of your voice. If he does, praise him. Most dogs will respond properly.

The next phase of COME WHEN CALLED is teaching your dog to SIT once he reaches you, after obeying the first part of the command. The effect is to break up the teaching process into three separate stages, COME, SIT, and STAY. Do not forget to praise the dog after he obeys each of these commands.

1. Repeat the first six steps for teaching COME WHEN CALLED.

2. Place the dog in a SIT-STAY. Praise him.

3. Command him to COME. Praise him.

4. Command him to SIT. Praise him.

5. Command him to STAY. Praise him.

6. Repeat each of these steps until the dog goes into a proper SIT position every time he comes to you on command.

COME WHEN CALLED concludes this *basic* obedience course for Golden Retrievers. By following these instructions you will definitely be able to control your dog and enrich the quality of your relationship. It should be noted, however, that obedience training can go much farther than the course offered here.

Dog obedience training is a sophisticated hobby, sport, and socially important function. The six obedience commands taught here are an introduction to this important activity.

Golden Retrievers of all ages should maintain a high state of discipline with continuing education and refresher courses. Certainly, practicing all that was learned from this chapter on a continuing basis will keep you and your dog happy.

We encourage you to continue your dog's education with a more complete dog training book; by entering a training class; by engaging the services of a professional dog trainer; or by joining a club focused on the sport of obedience trials, many of which are sponsored by the American Kennel Club and the United Kennel Club.

Training a dog is satisfying and rewarding. Training a dog is also fun.

CHAPTER NINE

Solving Behavior Problems

When Golden families tell dog stories, they almost never complain about behavior problems because they consider everything their dog does funny, lovable, and excusable. Although *typical* Goldens are not problem dogs, they do offer the inexperienced dog owner behavior challenges that come as a surprise. The good news is that the few behavior problems typical of the breed are not difficult to correct and change if you know what to expect.

Golden Retrievers are very oral. If given the opportunity, they will happily munch on your books (hardcovers seem to taste best) or anything else they can gnaw on, including a stack of envelopes with your monthly bills and payments inside. They especially enjoy the flavor of rare books and record albums, the more expensive the better. CDs and videotapes are high on the list of delicacies. *Word of mouth* means something else to Golden Retrievers. Let us not forget their method of retrieving.

As puppies they will nip your fingers and mouth anything until it is saturated and drenched with saliva. They like to dig. It doesn't matter whether you have a splendid lawn, an unpaved backyard, or just a small patch of grass on the side of the house; most Goldens can be counted on to dig holes into the entire surface. And they especially like to jump on you if you are wearing a white outfit or a spotless suit just back from the dry cleaner.

The new owner will be relieved to know that most of the behavior problems of Golden Retrievers can be avoided with prevention techniques and mild corrections employed as early as possible. Any behavior pattern exhibited by a puppy should be evaluated by the

Golden Retrievers are angels and would never do a thing to upset their families . . . or would they?

owner, who must consider whether or not it will be acceptable when the dog becomes an adult. For example, a cute eight-week-old puppy jumping on its owner's knee to be petted or picked up may not be so cute when it is a seventy-five-pound grown dog with muddy paws. A new owner must show foresight when raising a puppy or spend the next twelve years correcting behavior that could have been avoided.

The most common behavior problems of Golden Retrievers are *chewing, digging, jumping on people, mouthing*, and *nipping*. Here are suggestions for solving these problems.

Chewing

Of all the behavior problems of dogs, destructive chewing is the most upsetting, even more so than housebreaking mistakes. A mess on the carpet can be cleaned up. But when the arm is chewed off a leather couch, your only options are to live with it or buy another one. Not only is chewing behavior exasperating, it is expensive and at times very upsetting. When a dog chews up a stamp collection or an antique, he has probably destroyed years of effort and expense. Many a new dog owner has lost a personal treasure to the teeth of dogs that chewed up the home. A dog with a chewing problem will damage furniture, curtains, appliances, books, shoes, clothing, and anything else available for him to sink his teeth into, including doors, walls, and baseboards. Some dog owners have lost hundreds and sometimes thousands of dollars in personal possessions. A canine chewer does not win the hearts and minds of his family. This unhappiness and disappointment can be avoided with a little knowledge and effort. Chewing problems are not difficult to solve.

Creating an aversion to chewing your possessions is the most effective way to stop this behavior. It's easy. Simply make your stuff taste awful. The best way to do this is to mix a thick paste consisting of alum powder and water. (Alum powder can be bought over the counter at any drugstore and is inexpensive.) Mix the powder with a small amount of water until it is the consistency of mustard. Smear the mixture on the dog's favorite chewing items. The alum paste does not stain and washes off easily. It tastes unpleasantly bitter and has a contracting, puckering effect on a dog's tongue and mouth. It makes destructive chewing an unappealing experience. Although alum is not harmful if eaten, it should be used in small quantities. The mixture could upset a dog if swallowed in large quantities. Given its unpleasant taste, it is unlikely that a dog will lick very much of it.

Do not confine your pet improperly. Some dogs will chew anything and everything in an attempt to escape or relieve their emotional stress if they are confined in a room behind a closed door. Most will whimper, bark, and eventually chew on whatever they can find. If a dog is left alone behind a closed door, his chewing behavior may become frantic and destructive.

An untrained dog with a chewing problem can be very destructive when left alone.

An untrained dog with or without a chewing problem should *not* have the run of the house when left alone. He should be confined properly. See Puppygate, page 72.

Most chewing problems start in puppyhood, when they are easily prevented from becoming serious. If your puppy starts to chew on any of your possessions, discourage him immediately by saying, "NO," in a firm tone of voice. Praise the dog immediately afterward and give him a chew toy made of nylon or rawhide to gnaw on. This redirects the chewing behavior away from your possessions. Do not allow your puppy to chew on anything that remotely resembles furniture, clothing, carpeting, curtains, or things you value. Never give your dog an old shoe or a knotted towel to chew on, because sooner or later he will look for the good stuff. Avoid dog toys such as a latex pork chop or a rolled newspaper. Give him a nylon or rawhide chew toy or a large, hard ball that he can call his own.

The chewing behavior of puppies is almost always caused by teething. This will continue well into the dog's first year. Soak several washcloths in cold water, squeeze them, stretch them into rope shape, and freeze them. When they are cold and hard, give them to your dog to chew on, one at a time. Each one will stay cold for at least sixty minutes. As he chews on them, the coldness will numb his gums and ease his pain.

Some dogs chew because of the emotional stress they experience when left alone, or because they are bored, or because chewing has become a habit ignored as a puppy. It is a popular misconception that dogs chew destructively for spite or to punish their owners for leaving them alone. This is incorrect. Spite and revenge are based on human feelings and thoughts.

Never punish a dog with a chewing problem. It is counterproductive and changes nothing except to add to his emotional stress. If you understand what makes your dog chew, you are more likely to correct the problem by changing the conditions that have caused it. Play a soft radio in the background when he is alone. Give him many chew toys with which to distract himself.

If all else fails, you can give your dog a correction, but only if you actually catch him in the act of chewing. Considering the sensitivity of Golden Retrievers, a verbal correction, "NO," is usually effective. A particularly stubborn dog may require a leash correction. Read the entire first portion of Chapter 8, "Obedience-Training Your Golden Retriever."

Digging

All dogs will dig up your yard or front lawn if you give them the opportunity, but some breeds like to do it more than others. Goldens love to dig and roll in the soft ground. They delight in sinking their paws into the dirt and scattering it everywhere. Because of this, Golden puppies should be supervised when allowed outdoors so that any attempt to dig is greeted with a firm "NO" and a tossed toy to divert the dog's attention. Do not leave your puppy outside, unattended, on a soft surface. Put him in an exercise pen sitting on concrete or on grass with chicken wire spread over the bottom.

The correct use of chicken wire is one of the best self-correcting methods available. Most dogs are drawn to the same holes they dug before, even if they are filled in with the original dirt. Fill your dog's favorite hole with a layer of chicken wire close to the surface and cover it with dirt. This makes it unpleasant for digging. You can also fill in the existing holes with large rocks. They are unpleasant for the dog to dig his paws into and discourage him from digging further.

Chicken wire is not only the best filler, it is also the best deterrent when used to cover the ground the dog likes to dig in. Use it in three- to six-foot lengths and cover it with a thin coating of dirt. If your dog moves his digging activities to another location, cover that with chicken wire, too. Do not let him see you laying the wire or he will dig in another location and fail to undergo the self-teaching experience. The idea is to make digging as difficult and disagreeable as possible. If you correct the problem in puppyhood, you will avoid serious consequences when the dog is fully grown.

Jumping on People

Few dogs are as enthusiastic as Golden Retrievers when they greet someone. Their energized expressions of affection are sweet and funny, unless you happen to be wearing your best clothes and are ready for a night out or an important meeting. When a full-grown Golden Retriever jumps on you, he will smudge your clothing with whatever is on his paws and wrinkle your freshly pressed outfit. If you are wearing makeup, he will smear it as he slurps your face.

Even obedience-trained dogs jump up on people if they are not consistently corrected every time they do it. Goldens are so affectionate and enthusiastic that they will jump on anyone they like whether they are out on the street or at home. They like to jump on people as a way of saying how happy they are to see them. This is also how they tell you they want to play, eat, or get some attention.

Sooner or later even the nicest dog that is allowed to jump on people will create an unpleasant situation. While many people enjoy a dog's attention, some are frightened when jumped on, especially children. Being jumped on by a dog makes some people angry. You cannot expect a dog to know the difference between who likes it and who doesn't. The no-jumping rule should apply at all times and in every situation. Either the dog is allowed to jump on everyone or he is allowed to jump on no one. There can be no in-between here without confusing the dog and frustrating the family.

When the various members of the family are inconsistent about the dog's jumping, it encourages this behavior to continue. Do not allow the dog to jump up on you when you feel playful and then disallow it when you are not up for it. This is confusing and unfair. You can stop your dog from jumping only if you are diligent about correcting him *every time* he jumps on someone, including yourself. Before attempting to deal with this behavior, you must ask yourself if you want your dog to stop jumping on people. If the answer is yes, please continue.

Teaching your dog *not* to jump on people is easy. It simply requires a correction whenever he jumps. If applied properly, a leash correction (the corrective jerk) solves the problem. Read the entire first portion of Chapter 8, "Obedience-Training Your Golden Retriever," with particular attention to The Corrective Jerk.

The leash correction is best for correcting jumping behavior. Dogs usually jump on their owners when they come home or when they see people they like. Place the leash and training collar on your dog, and set up a similar situation in which another member of the household walks through the door and you are prepared to grab the leash and make the correction. When the dog jumps on the person coming through the door, jerk the leash firmly to the right, and at the same time say, "NO," in a firm tone of voice. The firmness of the jerk and the force of your voice must be appropriate for the age and temperament of your dog. Obviously, a puppy or sensitive dog must be handled with less vigor than a typical adult dog. Stubborn dogs should be corrected with the shake-can technique offered on the next page.

Praise the dog immediately for responding to the correction (even if his response was not perfect). Praise immediately following a correction is of vital importance. The dog will probably jump up again if you make yourself available. (Do not invite him to jump on you, though.) The instant he does, give him another leash correction accompanied with a firm "NO." Always use the firm "NO" as part of any correction so that eventually the verbal correction alone will suffice. Correct the dog each time he jumps on you or anyone else and he will eventually change his ways.

Stubborn dogs that do not respond properly to a leash correction require a noise correction with the use of a simple improvised training tool called the shake can. Take an empty soda can, wash it, and slip ten pennies into it. Tape the opening so the pennies cannot fall out. Now shake the can vigorously. It will make a very commanding rattle similar to the sound of a New Year's Eve noisemaker. This is an ideal way to correct an obstinate dog. It easily gets his attention when shaken loudly and accompanied with a very firm "NO!" It also enables you to deliver a correction anytime and anyplace because it does not require a leash and training collar.

For a number of reasons it is important to hold the shake can behind your back when you use it. The rattling sound can be too startling even for a stubborn dog or puppy. Making a dog fearful is very unkind and not the basis for a good relationship. Creating fear should never be a part of dog training or problem solving. Also, by shaking the can behind your back you will avoid creating fearful associations with your hand movements or gestures. The rattling sound simply serves as a background noise to your loud, firm "NO!" The most important aspect of any correction is the word "NO" sharply delivered in a firm tone of voice. The rattling sound is used to back up your voice and get the dog's attention. Eventually, the dog will always respond properly to a simple "NO" from you or the members of your family.

For very sensitive dogs and puppies, use a small squirt bottle of water as a corrective tool rather than the leash and collar or shake can. The squirt bottle should be the kind used to spray houseplants, etcetera. Hold it behind your back. When the dog jumps on you, spray him gently in the face with one quick sprinkle of water. As you do, say, "NO," in a firm tone of voice. Do not forget to praise the dog immediately after. The squirt bottle is effective yet gentle.

To avoid the problem entirely, do not allow your puppy to jump on you, even though he is cute and adorable. If you correct him when he tries it, he will never do it as an adult dog.

Assuming the dog has been obedience-trained, he should be commanded to "SIT" immediately following any correction. Praise the dog after he obeys the command. If he has *not* been obedience-trained, then the corrective jerk is all you can use until the dog is brought under control through training. He may still try to jump after the first jerk. Correct the dog every time he jumps until he stops.

Dogs that jump on people always indulge in this upsetting behavior while outside for a walk. When it happens, the tendency for dog owners is to pull the dog away. Instead, give him a corrective jerk, a firm "NO," and enthusiastic praise for jumping down. Immediately, turn and swiftly walk in the opposite direction. Perform this sequence every time the dog jumps on someone while out for a walk and the problem will end.

Bear in mind that the problem will continue forever if you, your family, your friends, or neighbors allow the dog to jump on them at any time. Make it clear to everyone that he must never be invited to jump on them or encouraged by petting him or giving him any form of approval for this unwanted behavior.

A word of caution. Do not knock your dog off you with a hard knee to his chest in order to stop him from jumping. Do not step on his toes for this or any other reason. Do not use force of any kind to push the dog off you. These gestures are not only painful, they are medically dangerous.

Using training techniques that hurt your dog destroys the chances of having a happy, satisfying relationship with him. They could make your dog aggressive with strangers and shy with you. No right-thinking person uses pain to teach a child anything, so why would anyone do that to a loving, trusting dog? Training techniques based on pain are ineffective and harmful to the dog's personality. To solve the problem of jumping on people, be consistent in your use of the correction techniques offered here as they are needed.

Mouthing and Nipping

Mouthing

This seemingly harmless activity is usually not recognized as a be-havior problem and, as a matter of fact, is often thought of as cute. However, when a puppy (or adult dog) *mouths*, he puts his open mouth on your hand, your arm, your leg, or anything that belongs to you, including any and all of your possessions. This behavior quickly loses its charm as your clothing begins to soak with your dog's saliva and your possessions become seriously damaged from the saturation and the teeth marks. The worst result of mouthing is its progression into a nipping and biting problem.

Nipping

Everyone smiles when puppies take fingers into their mouths and nibble on them like Ritz crackers. No one seems to realize that this is a sneak preview of biting problems. A nip from a puppy usually in-volves the front teeth and feels like a slight pinch without full pres-sure. The nip may or may not be painful, but that is not the point.

Unfortunately, nipping is not considered to be a behavior problem by dog owners until the nipper turns into a biter.

Mouthing and nipping problems can be attributed to the oral inclinations of Retrievers, to first-year teething pain, and to the wrong kind of stimulation from the dog's family.

As with human babies, teething is characterized by soreness and itching of the gums, along with some slight bleeding and drooling. When puppies and young dogs teethe, all of their energy and concentration become focused on relieving the discomfort of their gums by chewing, nipping, and mouthing. If allowed to go uncorrected, this behavior becomes generalized and habitual.

Breed characteristics of the Golden Retriever must be considered part of the problem. Retrievers were bred to carry fallen birds back to their human hunting partners *in their mouth*. It is instinctive for Retrievers and other bird dogs to express themselves with oral behavior.

Owner-induced behavior is often the cause of nipping and mouthing. Playing aggressive games such as tug-of-war with an old sock or tennis shoe in a puppy's teeth, with seemingly humorous pulling and growling, encourages mouthing, nipping, and, eventually, biting. Boxing and wrestling with your dog has the same effect. Placing your fingers in the dog's mouth as a form of amusement also creates these problems. Hitting your dog can induce him to fight back with his teeth. Pushing him away with your hands can inspire your puppy to nip at you. When you are grooming your dog or giving him medicine, he will nip or mouth if you hurt him. If what you do with your hands causes pain, your dog will nip and mouth you until it becomes a more serious behavior problem. A puppy should never be allowed to use his teeth on any human being for any reason.

Mouthing and Nipping Solutions

Teething. When mouthing and nipping are caused by teething, the solution is to alleviate the dog's pain and discomfort. Soak several washcloths in cold water. Twist them and put them in the freezer.

Once they are frozen, give them to the puppy one at a time as a chew toy. Each frozen washcloth will stay cold for at least sixty minutes. The coldness will numb the dog's gums and ease his pain. Another possibility is to freeze an entire bowl of water and allow the dog to lick it all day long. Chew toys are also beneficial. Use hard rubber toys, rawhide bones, and synthetic bones made of hard, digestible nylon.

Corrections. Correcting your dog when you catch him nipping or mouthing is the most effective method of stopping this unwanted behavior and preventing it from becoming permanent. There are three types of acceptable corrections: verbal corrections, shake-can corrections, and leash corrections.

Verbal corrections. Reprimand the dog by saying, "NO," in a firm tone of voice. Given the sensitivity of Golden Retrievers, this will be effective for most puppies and dogs. Following the correction, praise your dog lavishly and redirect his desire to chew with a substitute chew toy.

Shake-can corrections. This is an alternative for dogs that do not respond to your verbal corrections. The shake can is a homemade training tool that works when your dog is not wearing a leash and collar. Take several empty soda cans, wash them, and slip ten pennies into each one. Tape the opening so the pennies cannot fall out. When you shake the can vigorously it will make a loud, commanding rattle. It is meant to get your dog's attention and give him a negative message.

Place the shake cans in the areas where your dog is likely to nip or mouth. When he misbehaves, shake the can behind your back and say, "NO," in a firm tone of voice. After each correction praise him lavishly and give him a substitute chew toy.

Leash corrections. See The Corrective Jerk in Chapter 8, "Obedience-Training Your Golden Retriever," (page 107). Leash corrections are an important training tool when all else fails. Of all the corrections this is the most effective one for dogs that do not respond to anything else.

Correct the dog with a quick little jerk of the leash, but only when he is actually nipping or mouthing.

After each correction praise your dog and give him a chew toy or nylon bone as a substitution for your hand.

It is unusual for an adult Golden to nip, but many are *mouthy* and as a matter of instinct will gently take your arm in their mouth when happy to see you. This should be discouraged with a mild correction.

Keeping Your Golden Retriever Healthy

Devoted dog owners can give their pets a happy, vigorous life with preventive medicine, healthcare, and common sense. When anticipating the Golden years, it is hard to envision the possibility of your dog being sick. Nevertheless, it is unrealistic to avoid the subject entirely. In the war against sickness, information is the most potent weapon; a veterinarian is the greatest ally; and preventive medicine is the most effective strategy.

Vaccinations

Vaccinations are the foundation of preventive medicine. When it comes to saving the lives of dogs, antiviral and antibacterial vaccines are the most significant weapons available against disease. Millions of dogs have been spared the effects of debilitating sickness and painful death because of the immunities provided by vaccinations.

Vaccines are preparations of *killed* or *modified live* (weakened) strains of disease-causing agents that are injected into the body. They stimulate the immune system and promote the formation of antibodies, which attack and kill specific viruses or bacteria. It is like fighting fire with fire. Vaccines are intended to create immunity to the specific diseases they introduce into the body. Please note: A very small number of vaccinated animals do not get full immunity from every vaccine. Most vaccinated dogs, however, achieve full immunity and avoid the diseases for which they have been immunized.

When a puppy is first born, it receives *colostrum* with the first feedings of mother's milk. *Colostrum* creates a population of antibodies in the newborn puppy that fight disease for the first four to six weeks of life. This protection, however, is temporary, and while active in the body it interferes with the effectiveness of most vaccines that may be introduced. Consequently, puppies are not vaccinated until they are weaned from mother's milk at approximately six weeks of age. The vaccine for *kennel cough (Bordetella bronchiseptica)* is an exception and puppies as young as two weeks of age may be vaccinated for this.

Depending upon the veterinarian's point of view, the breeder, and the nature of the vaccines used, puppies may be vaccinated at six, eight, twelve, sixteen, or perhaps twenty weeks of age. They are usually vaccinated with a combination of vaccines that must be repeated every year. Puppies and dogs can be vaccinated for canine distemper, infectious canine hepatitis, rabies, canine parvovirus, and kennel cough in combination with vaccines for leptospirosis, canine coronavirus, and Lyme disease (Lyme borreliosis). *All dogs must be given annual "booster shots" (yearly vaccinations) for the rest of their life if they are to maintain immunity.*

The Annual Checkup

Many medical problems are prevented, or at least caught early, at a dog's annual medical examination. It is essential for pet owners to understand the importance of a complete annual checkup for their dogs. A typical veterinary examination should include looking at both ears, the nose, mouth, teeth, throat, respiratory system, spine or musculoskeletal system, skin, legs, abdominal cavity, cardiovascular system, anal area, and genitalia. An annual checkup is the time to have your dog vaccinated for the first time or revaccinated with booster shots. If your dog is sick or the veterinarian suspects a possible medical problem, she or he may ask for one or more laboratory tests involving stool samples, blood tests, or X-rays.

Exercise

Exercise is an important means of preventing sickness and promoting good health. Golden Retrievers working in the field by the side of hunters on a regular basis stay in good shape and get more than their share of exercise. Dogs living as pets, however, must be exercised and allowed to express their energetic exuberance or become vulnerable to medical problems associated with lethargy and boredom. Exercise for dogs can simply be a few games, a walk, a run, a swim, or anything that involves exertion. Maintaining good muscle tone is important, but most of all, exercising a Golden Retriever should be fun. It also strengthens the loving bond between the dog and his family.

In general terms, a dog's need for exercise should be based on the physical activity for which its breed was created. Specifically, a Golden Retriever is a strong, muscular, and energetic dog born to

Bar jumps in agility and obedience trials are good exercise. Other important forms of exercise are walking, swimming, running, and retrieval games with a ball or stick.

run, leap, swim, and scurry back to you with a bird in its soft mouth. Golden Retrievers are dogs with a great need to use their strength and energy. Exercise is important not only for the body but for dogs' mental stability and happiness as well. Goldens that never get to run or swim go through life unfulfilled. While it is not necessary for Goldens living as pets to go hunting, they must have energy-consuming activities *with their family* that give them a sense of pleasure and purpose.

Dogs that are gently exercised as puppies develop better than those that aren't. Most dogs are considered middle-aged at seven years because that is when their metabolic system begins to slow down. The food they consume converts more readily to fat unless it is burned off in some form of physical activity. Golden Retrievers, especially those living in cities, should be given one or more walks a day, a good run (depending on their age), and some vigorous play time.

A puppy needs only ten or twenty minutes of exercise several times a day. The best exercise for puppies is free play with another dog or several toys and a human. Even at the earliest age, games involving retrieving are best. Retriever puppies stop playing when they get tired and know when to rest.

A young dog should get at least thirty minutes of walking, running, playing, or jogging once or twice a day. *Do not jog with a puppy. Do not run dogs of any age while on a bicycle, with or without a leash attached.* A dog must never be dragged by the leash or put in danger of getting in front of the wheels of any moving vehicle.

Middle-aged and older dogs must also be exercised but with more moderation and caution than with younger dogs. Gentle walks, carefully thrown balls, and games of your own invention are best.

Never exercise a dog immediately after he has eaten. Large dogs are prone to *bloat*, a life-threatening medical condition that can be brought about from strenuous activity immediately following a meal.

Take your puppy or adult dog for walks on a regular basis as often as possible, even if it's only for an errand. An occasional weekend of exercise is worse than none at all because it can strain the body, especially on an older dog. Consistency is the most important and beneficial aspect of exercise. Giving your adult dog a long, hard run once a day or several times a week is also beneficial.

Playing fetch with a Frisbee will please any dog, especially a Golden Retriever. You can get the same enjoyable effect, though, from a large ball or a stick. Use almost anything that promotes a run-and-fetch game. However, do not use a tennis ball because it can lodge in the throat or be chewed into pieces, both of which have obvious consequences.

Grooming and Hygiene

Essential elements of good health are hygiene and grooming. These go far to prevent sickness and disease. This section does not cover the intricacies of dog grooming for its own sake. Entire books exist for that purpose and dog grooming salons are available everywhere for the dog owner desiring that service. In this section grooming as it applies to hygiene is the concern. A limited grooming effort is necessary to maintain good health for all Golden Retrievers. For the necessary equipment see Grooming Tools in Chapter 5, "Golden Gear (What Your Dog Needs)."

The Golden Retriever coat

The coat consists of dense, water-repellent fur of medium-to-long length. It is neither hard nor silky and lies flat against the body; it may be straight or somewhat wavy. The hair feathers out on the back of the front legs up to the thighs, on the neck, and underneath the tail, forming an attractive plume.

Brushing and combing

Goldens are expected to have a natural look with little or no clipping of the coat at all. However, they should be brushed at least twice a week (or more) to maintain luster and to prevent the fur from matting into uncontrollable tangles and clumps. A pin brush is best for this purpose. Brushing and then combing keeps the coat clean and stimulates the skin. Brushing and combing your Golden every week is more for the sake of good hygiene than for good looks. It is an opportunity to place loving hands on your pet as you check for tumors, abrasions, injuries, fleas, ticks, and other signs of poor health.

Baths

Goldens do not require baths unless they are unusually dirty or odorous. Bathing your pet twice a year is sufficient unless the dog is going to be shown or enter one of the competitive dog sports. Frequent brushing and combing avoids the need for repeated baths.

Nails

A Golden's nails should be clipped when they are no longer even with the surface of the paw pad. Neglected nails, if not worn down naturally from hard surfaces, can throw a dog off balance and irritate the paw. Use a guillotine-type nail trimmer, holding it vertically while holding the dog's paw up to it. Insert the protruding nail into the circular opening. Trim away a small amount of nail at a time until you are confident enough to snip off the nail in one slice. Do not trim too close to the *quick*, which is a thin, red-to-pink vein, or the nail will bleed. A good rule to follow is to cut at the point where the nails begin to curve. If the nail should bleed, apply an antiseptic coagulant powder or styptic pencil, which can be purchased at any drug store or pet supply store.

Ears

Long-coated dogs such as the Golden Retriever accumulate long hairs in the ear canal that eventually become matted and provide a painful area for infection or flea infestation. Ear powders are available that harden the hairs and make them easy to pluck out with your fingers. Ears should be kept clean and free of wax deposits with a cloth wrapped around your finger or with a cotton swab dipped in baby oil or peroxide. Do not penetrate too deep into the canal to avoid causing an injury. If the hair is matted or tangled within the ear, it is best to have a professional groomer or veterinarian handle the situation.

Teeth

Oral hygiene is as important to pets as it is to humans and should not be overlooked. It is desirable to clean your dog's teeth at least once a week to avoid extensive veterinary dental treatment. Most pets require sedation or anesthesia for thorough dental treatment.

Canine dental tools, toothbrushes, and cleaning agents designed for dogs are available in most pet supply stores and catalogs. Baking soda mixed into a paste with water is just as effective. You may use a clean washcloth to scrub your dog's teeth, providing there is little hardened plaque accumulated on the surfaces. Under no circumstance should toothpaste meant for humans be used on a dog. It can be harmful. Ask your veterinarian about regular care of your dog's teeth.

CHAPTER ELEVEN

Canine Medical Conditions

Keeping your dog in good health requires an understanding of when he is in bad health. It is essential for dog owners to have some basis for knowing when something is wrong. This uncomplicated information is important to have. It can be of great value when the question of taking your dog to a veterinarian arises.

It is not difficult to know when your dog is sick if you know what is normal and what is abnormal for him. Annual checkups help a great deal, but knowing your dog's normal physical condition, behavior, and body language are of greater help. When your dog is sick, he will require medical attention. Knowing when to take your dog to a veterinarian could save his life.

Signs and Symptoms of Canine Sickness

Limping
Loss of balance
Paralysis
Difficulty moving the neck or back
Difficulty changing body position
Listlessness, lethargy, passiveness
Loss of appetite
Unusual increase in appetite
Excessive weight gain or loss
Fever (normal range is 100°F to 102.5°F)
Vomiting
Prolonged diarrhea

Excessive thirst
Prolonged lack of thirst
Head shaking
Swiping ears with paws
Increased urination
Inability to urinate
Painful urination
Discolored urine (pink, red, dark yellow, or orange)
Loss of urinary control, especially in sleeping area
Coughing
Troublesome, labored, or inconsistent breathing
Pale or discolored gums
Abnormal scratching
Hair loss
Changes of skin tone (redness, sores, lumps, openings, crusts, scales, discharges, or changes of color)
Seizures
Bleeding
Inflammation of the eyes
Excessive tearing
Excessive sneezing
Constant nasal discharge
Mouth odor
Inability to chew
Whimpering

Serious Canine Infectious Diseases

Although *The Golden Years* is not a medical manual, it would be a serious omission and a disservice to fail to provide information about the medical conditions included here. The following diseases are very serious and, in many cases, life-threatening. They cannot be diagnosed or treated by anyone other than a veterinarian. Nevertheless, recognizing the early signs of disease and getting swift veterinary attention can be of significant value. The information is presented here to help dog owners understand the seriousness of these diseases so that they can give their dogs the best chance for survival.

Canine Distemper

This highly contagious disease is caused by a virus similar to the one that causes measles in humans. Reports indicate that canine distemper, worldwide, is the leading cause of death from infectious disease in dogs. It is seen most commonly in puppies between three and eight months of age, especially if they have not been vaccinated. At this age young dogs are weaned and can no longer benefit from the protection provided by *colostrum*, which creates a population of natural antibodies and is present in mothers' milk.

Signs

Canine distemper effects several areas of the body, including the respiratory system, the intestines, the skin, and the brain. Secondary infections are common and they can result in death. The first sign of distemper appears approximately three to fifteen days after exposure. Because the early signs are very subtle, symptoms may not be apparent for two to three weeks.

Stage 1: Signs are similar to those of human upper respiratory infections, including high fever, loss of appetite, and watery discharge from the eyes and nose. This can be accompanied with a dry, hacking cough. Diarrhea may also be present, leading to dehydration. Secondary infections such as skin lesions or even pneumonia may develop.

Stage 2: Brain involvement may be seen after two to three weeks of infection. Periods of head shaking, chewing motions, and slobbering may be observed. Epileptic-like seizures may occur. The infected dog may also move in uncontrollable circles as it kicks and yelps. These symptoms are followed by confusion and aimless walking, with no recognition of anyone familiar. The prognosis for dogs with brain involvement is usually death.

A secondary bacterial infection that sometimes results from distemper is called "hard pad"; it attacks the skin of the feet and nose. The pads form thick callus-like growths and the nose becomes thickened and horn-like. When this condition develops, there usually are accompanying signs of encephalitis.

Treatment

Prevention is the only real help. Immunization early in a puppy's life plus annual booster shots offers the best hope. Antibiotics are not effective against canine distemper but are given to support the secondary involvement of bacterial infections. Intravenous fluids are given to prevent dehydration. Anticonvulsants and sedatives are administered to control seizures. Medication is given to control diarrhea. The success of your veterinarian's treatment depends on the speed with which the dog receives professional care and the strength of the dog to fight off the virus.

Infectious Canine Hepatitis

Infectious canine hepatitis is a viral disease that is highly contagious and transmitted only to dogs. It affects the liver, the lining of the blood vessels, and the kidneys. It is a major cause of death in puppies and young dogs that are not vaccinated. The virus is passed from all body secretions of carrier dogs and is present in the urine of dogs several months after recovery. Dogs of all ages are susceptible. Infection is caused by ingesting contaminated material.

Signs

Hepatitis has a wide range of symptoms that can vary from mild at the beginning to furious episodes leading ultimately to death. In some cases, the signs of hepatitis are confused with those of canine distemper. The first sign is fever, often above 104°F, which may subside after twenty-four to forty-eight hours. Occasionally, a fever that lasts only one or two days is the sole sign of the disease, although blood tests reveal a low leukocyte count. In some cases the fever lasts longer than three or four days. Other signs include increased thirst, lack of appetite, depression, and excessive watering of the eyes and nose. Diarrhea, vomiting, spasms, and heavy and rapid breathing are also signs of this painful disease.

Puppies are very susceptible in the first few months of life, although dogs of any age can contract the virus. Shortly after exposure the virus is secreted in the urine, saliva, and stool. It is in this stage that the dog is most contagious. Even dogs that are recuperating can shed the virus for months afterward. In the extreme, fatal form puppies can die without obvious illness. Some infected dogs become ill suddenly with bloody diarrhea, collapse, and die. In the acute form the dog suffers with aggravated diarrhea, loss of appetite, and high fever. Other symptoms of the disease are photophobia (sensitivity to light), jaundice (yellowing of the eyes), and swelling of the liver characterized by a tucked-up appearance of the belly and accompanied by painful movements. In its mildest form the dog may only show loss of appetite, be lethargic, or just appear to be having a bad day.

Treatment

Blood tests can determine the diagnosis. If the disease is uncomplicated, it will run its course within one week with professional care. In such a case the dog will probably remain in the hospital or with the veterinarian for at least seven days. There is no therapy, however, for the disease itself. Treatment can only minimize the effects of shock and hemorrhaging, and prevent secondary bacterial infection. The attending vet may introduce intravenous fluid therapy, blood transfusions, and antibiotics as well as corticosteroids. The only defense against infectious canine hepatitis is early vaccination and annual boosters, which are important because there is no permanent immunity.

Rabies

Rabies is a fatal disease threatening all warm-blooded animals. In most industrialized countries throughout the world, cases of rabies involving humans have been eliminated almost entirely as the result of effective vaccination programs aimed at domestic dogs and cats. Incidents of rabies infecting dogs and cats are reported in relatively low numbers but nevertheless serve as a frightening reminder that this deadly disease is far from being eradicated. In the United States animals transmitting the disease are primarily skunks, raccoons, wild foxes, bats, and woodchucks (the only rodents involved to any great extent).

The rabies virus is spread through contact with saliva from an infected animal. This is usually transmitted through a bite. Saliva can also transmit the disease if it comes in direct contact with an open wound or through mucous membrane tissue (the lining of internal surfaces of the body, such as the mouth, digestive tract, respiratory tract, and urinary tract).

Incubation averages between three and eight weeks, but there have been cases with incubation as short as one week or as long as one year. The virus is carried quickly to the central nervous system. It reaches the spinal cord within four to five days and travels upward until it ultimately infects the brain. During this period it also travels to the salivary gland and can then be transmitted to another animal when bitten.

Signs

Rabies has two stages, the "furious" and the "dumb." The furious form lasts approximately one week and is identified by behavioral changes, including restlessness and characteristics contrary to the dog's personality, such as irritability, high energy in a normally sedate dog, or lethargy in a normally energetic dog. Friendly dogs become aggressive and shy. Shy dogs may become overly affectionate. Eventually the dog will avoid people, become aloof, and often stare off into space. A dog in the furious stage may also become ferocious and bite any person or animal that comes close.

Fever, nausea, and diarrhea are common. Dogs in this stage are sensitive to light and to being touched. Eventually they will chew violently on any restraint, such as a leash, or on the metal parts of their wire crate. In this condition the rabid dog, drooling, panting, frothing at the mouth as a result of rapid breathing through the saliva, may die from a convulsive seizure without progressing to the final, "dumb" stage, which takes the form of partial or total paralysis.

The dumb stage continues with diminishing aspects of the furious form as the head and neck muscles become paralyzed. The dog suffers. Mercifully, death ensues within one or two days.

Treatment

Rabies represents a fatal disease for dogs and humans, once the signs and symptoms become evident. It is highly dangerous to attempt treatment of rabid dogs because of the great risk of infection to health caregivers.

Humans can be treated *before* clinical signs appear. For this reason, *immediate* medical attention is required following a bite from an animal suspected of rabies. Once the symptoms become evident, the disease is usually fatal in dogs and humans alike.

All dog owners are advised to have their pets vaccinated for rabies at three months of age and again twelve months later. The dog should then be revaccinated every three years or as instructed by the manufacturers of the vaccine.

Parvovirus

"Parvo" is a highly contagious virus that is transmitted to the body orally by contact with infected feces and possibly through urine droplets. It can be carried on the bottom of shoes or transported on any other object. Dogs of any age can be affected, although puppies under the age of five months have the highest mortality rate. Elderly dogs are also more susceptible. This deadly disease is seen in two forms:

Parvoviral enteritis

This form enters the body through the oral cavity; it attacks the tonsils first and then is concentrated within the entire intestinal tract, impairing all normal functions of digestion and resulting in life-threatening loss of fluids and body weight.

Signs

The enteritis form causes unrelenting bloody diarrhea, painful vomiting, depression, and dehydration. Infected puppies will run high temperatures and older dogs will run unusually low temperatures. Other signs are severe coughing and swelling of the cornea of the eye. The onset of parvo is sudden and bewildering, and without immediate veterinary treatment the dog dies in a matter of days.

The incubation period is approximately seven to fourteen days after exposure. The first signs are severe depression and loss of appetite.

A second form of this deadly disease is parvoviral myocarditis.

Parvoviral myocarditis

This form is seen almost exclusively in puppies under three months of age. Myocarditis is an inflammation of the heart muscle that leads to heart failure and death and occurs in pups from nonimmune mothers. Puppies affected will stop nursing and develop difficulty breathing. Death usually occurs suddenly between the ages of three and eight weeks. This form of parvo has become rare because of routine vaccination of most dogs.

Treatment

There is no antiviral therapy for canine parvovirus available. Survival and treatment depend on the form of parvo contracted, the age of the dog, the severity of the infection, and how quickly the dog receives professional care. Prompt action by the pet owner is often a life-and-death factor.

The veterinarian's objective is to stabilize the dog until the body's immune system clears the infection. Massive fluid loss through diarrhea and vomiting is the principal cause of death. Therefore, replacement of body fluids plays a major role in recovery. Intravenous (IV) fluids and medications (administered through a vein) are essential in replacing fluid loss and controlling vomiting and diarrhea. Broad-spectrum antibiotics are given to prevent or fight secondary bacterial infections, such as pneumonia. Hospitalization is necessary.

Prevention begins with vaccination of the mother before pregnancy with modified live vaccine. Annual booster shots are necessary. If the puppies are vaccinated at too early an age, the antibodies from mother's milk will not only cause vaccine failure but will prevent them from developing their own active immune response. The first few months of life offer ample opportunity for parvovirus to develop.

If a dog or puppy becomes infected with parvovirus, separate it from other dogs in the household or kennel and minimize contact between sick and healthy animals. Clean all of the dog's areas with hot, soapy water to remove possibly infected litter and then disinfect with a 1:32 dilution of chlorine bleach and water to kill the persistent virus, which is not easily eradicated.

Canine Infectious Tracheobronchitis ("Kennel Cough")

This inflammation of the upper throat, trachea, and bronchi is a persistent illness that is viewed as a complex clinical syndrome produced by various infectious bacteria and viruses, at times in combination. Among them are:

Bordetella bronchiseptica, the most dominant infecting agent of the kennel cough complex. It is a bacterium that is capable of causing severe tracheobronchitis on its own without the invasion of other pathogens in the syndrome;

Canine parainfluenza virus, another element in the kennel cough complex. It is a virus belonging to the same family as canine distemper viruses and produces a mild to moderately severe infection in the windpipe and large air passages of the lungs;

Canine adenovirus-2, a DNA-containing virus that causes upper respiratory tract infections;

Mycoplasmas, microorganisms that are bacteria-like, inhabiting the respiratory and genital tracts of dogs. Parasitic in nature, they exist without cell walls and require no oxygen. They are considered to be a contributing factor to the kennel cough syndrome in some cases. They are capable of initiating upper respiratory disease on their own, in some rare instances;

Canine distemper virus, although a more severe disease producing intense systemic illness, has early signs almost impossible to distinguish from those of kennel cough;

Canine herpesvirus, a DNA virus that, like canine adenovirus-2, causes moderate upper respiratory tract infections;

Pasteurella multocida, a bacterium found in the upper respiratory tract that can contribute to the overall syndrome.

Signs

Although the signs vary depending upon the pathogen or combinations of pathogens involved, the first obvious sign is usually moist coughing and the release of sputum. After several days the cough becomes harsh, dry, and almost nonproductive and takes on a hacking, irritating quality, possibly caused by irritation of the vocal mechanism and the early stages of laryngitis. Almost anything will induce the sudden bouts of coughing, including emotional stress, excitement, even drinking water. In some extreme cases a discharge from the nose and eyes is present and may be followed by lethargy, fever, and loss of appetite. These signs begin to resemble the early stages of canine distemper. The cough will persist at its optimum for several weeks and decrease to a low-level cough for possibly one or two months. The signs of kennel cough are persistent, long-lived, and unpleasant for the dog and the humans surrounding him.

Treatment

Limited activity is advised; the dog should be kept warm, comfortable, and free of emotional stress. An environment without cold drafts is beneficial. In some cases antibiotics are recommended along with cough suppressant medications. Various drugs are also available to widen clogged airways, reduce inflammation, or break up mucous secretions within the airway and are prescribed by a veterinarian when appropriate. In extreme situations intravenous administration of fluids becomes necessary.

Vaccination for kennel cough is recommended but is not 100 percent effective in all dogs. Vaccines combining agents for *Bordetella bronchiseptica*, canine parainfluenza virus, and canine adenovirus-2 offer the best opportunity for protection. However, it is somewhat like vaccinating for the common cold.

A good prevention program must include keeping kennels and areas occupied by dogs meticulously clean and disinfected with various commercial products or with a chlorine bleach solution consisting of one part bleach to thirty-two parts water.

Canine Coronavirus Enteritis

This infectious enteritis can affect dogs of all ages, although young puppies and adult dogs in stress are at the greatest risk. Coronavirus infection can range from insignificant to life-threatening.

Signs
Varied, from mild infections to sudden death. Clinical signs may include loss of appetite, depression, vomiting, diarrhea, and dehydration. The feces may be loose, yellow-orange, and contain strands of blood or mucus. In some cases canine coronavirus enteritis is seen in combination with other pathogens, such as parvovirus.

Treatment
Similar to parvovirus. Veterinary care is required but is supportive rather than curative. Control of vomiting and diarrhea is necessary to prevent extreme fluid loss from the body. In some cases, intravenous replacement of fluids is necessary. Vaccine for coronavirus is available but should be given after evaluation by a veterinarian as to its practicality for a specific dog.

Internal Parasites

Almost all internal parasites that infect a dog's body are referred to as "worms." They vary in type, size, effect, and danger to the health of the dog. Although internal parasites can do harm to the dog's body, with early detection and treatment few create permanent or irreparable damage. When treated promptly, the infected dog returns to good health. Depending on the degree of infestation, the condition runs from mild to extremely serious.

Internal parasites are among the most common ailments of dogs and other animals. Almost all puppies have them, and adult dogs get them at one time or another. They must be treated as swiftly as possible by a veterinarian.

All worms have some signs in common that can alert the dog owner to get help for the dog. The early signs include a lethargic manner, inconsistent appetite, diarrhea, and blood in the stool. The signs of heavy infestation are loss of weight, bloated stomach, loss of fluid, dry and thinning coat, constant drowsiness, and anemia.

There are many species of internal parasites that infect dogs, but only the most common species are included in this limited segment.

Roundworms (Ascarids)

There is no parasite more common to dogs than roundworms. They are white and resemble spaghetti or earthworms. They are most often seen in the dog's stool or vomitus. The worms range in length from one to seven inches long. The eggs are protected by a hard shell and can live for long periods of time in the soil. The adult worm embeds in the intestinal tract and there deposits its eggs, then passes out of the body through the stool. If the eggs are then ingested by a host, the life cycle is completed and starts again. By eating the eggs in infested soil or fecal matter, the dog becomes infested. Ingestion of infested rodents, birds, and insects also allows entry to a host animal. Ascarids are very commonly found in newborn puppies because of the mother's infection during pregnancy, although the mother need not be infected for puppies to be invaded by these parasites. This happens when the dormant larvae from the mother become active and circulate through the blood system as well as getting into the breast milk. Most puppies are born with roundworms. Adult dogs seldom experience serious illness from ascarids. However, infection can be fatal for heavily infested puppies. All roundworm infestations must be treated quickly. Proper worming and good sanitation are the best preventive methods of control. Consult a veterinarian for diagnosis and treatment.

Children can also be infected with worms by ingesting contaminated soil or feces.

Hookworms (*Ancylostoma caninum*)

Hookworms fasten themselves to the wall of the intestine and draw blood from their host. They range in length from one-fourth to one-half inch long. Dogs acquire these worms from infected soil or feces. Immature worms migrate to the intestine, where they grow into adults. Eggs are passed into the stool in approximately two weeks, thus completing the cycle.

The majority of infections are found in puppies of two to eight weeks of age with infection from mothers' milk. The infestation can be life-threatening to puppies. Adult dogs are also vulnerable to infection, although not as seriously as puppies. Signs of major hookworm infestation are diarrhea, anemia, noticeable weight loss, and increasing fatigue. Stools become bloody, dark to black in color, and tar-like. Hookworm disease that causes severe anemia is a medical emergency requiring hospitalization and intense veterinary treatment possibly involving blood transfusions, medication to kill the larvae quickly, and therapies designed to attack migrating larvae remaining within the tissue.

Adults or puppies that recover will probably be carriers because of a small number of arrested larvae and eggs lodged in the tissue. Follow-up treatment is required.

Diagnosis is ascertained by microscopic identification of the eggs in the infected dog's feces. Normal treatment involves orally introduced anthelmintic medications prescribed by a veterinarian. Professional diagnosis and treatment are essential.

Whipworms (*Trichuris vulpis*)

Whipworms are serious parasites and somewhat difficult to detect. They are threadlike, with one end thicker than the other, giving the appearance of a whip. The worms are approximately two to three inches long and live in the large intestine (cecum), where they attach themselves to the inner walls along the tract from the cecum to the colon. Once whipworm eggs are ingested, they develop into larvae and then grow into adult worms in the large intestine. This takes approximately ten weeks, and they remain there up to sixteen months. During that period, the host animal slowly loses blood with accompanying loss of weight. Diarrhea becomes frequent, with evidence of blood in the stools of heavily infested dogs. Poor health becomes evident.

Diagnosis is made by microscopic examination of the stool. In difficult cases examinations must be repeated before the eggs can be detected. There are various forms of medication for whipworms, including tablets and intravenous injections, usually administered over a three-month period with additional stool examinations.

Tapeworms (*Dipylidium caninum*)

Tapeworm is common among dogs. The most common sources of infection are fleas; eating infected raw fish; and eating infected uncooked meat or animal parts. Lice can also be a source of tapeworm.

Tapeworms can vary in length from less than one inch to several feet long. Their bodies are segmented and can be found around the anal area, attached to the coat or the anus. Occasionally several segments pass into the stool, but the head always remains to form new links.

Infection by tapeworm can sometimes take a long time to detect. It can begin with digestive upsets, irregular appetite, weight loss, stomach discomfort, and poor coat condition. Diagnosis is made through examination of fecal matter, although this is sometimes ineffective. Detection is more commonly made by observation of segments in the dog's stool, bed, or anal area.

Treatment involves destroying the head within the host's body. Contact with intermediate hosts such as mice, rats, squirrels, and rabbits must be avoided. Medications are applied orally or by intravenous injection in several doses over a specified period of time. See a veterinarian for professional diagnosis and treatment.

Heartworms (*Dirofilaria immitis*)

Heartworm disease is a very serious illness for dogs and can be fatal if not treated promptly and properly. Heartworms are large worms that lodge in the right side of the heart and in the pulmonary vessels of the lung. Because of this, the heart has to work much harder to pump blood to the lungs and places a damaging strain on the entire circulatory system. Eventually, the heart weakens and insufficient blood flow affects almost every other vital organ in the body.

The carrier of heartworm disease is the mosquito, which is the transmitter of the parasite during its larval stage. The female heartworm, while in the host dog's body, produces great quantities of moving embryos called microfilaria. Mosquitoes living on the blood of a host dog ingest the microfilaria, which remain in the mosquitoes' bodies for fourteen to twenty-one days and are then transmitted to the body of the next dog the mosquitoes bite. The heartworms enter the next victim's body in their larval stage by the mosquito's injection and then take five to six months to develop into mature worms.

The signs of an infected dog are exhaustion, coughing, loss of weight despite good diet and appetite, and breathing difficulties. Chronic cough brought about by strenuous exercise is the first symptom of a classic case. Death, in the advanced stage, may be brought about by collapse during severe exercise.

Veterinarians are now able to prevent heartworms with routinely prescribed medications for several months prior to the mosquito season and several months afterward. Blood tests prior to administration of this preventive medication are usual.

External Parasites

Fleas, flies, ticks, and lice are the carriers of disease, allergies, and, in some cases, internal parasites. When a dog's body is infected by external parasites, a veterinarian can best determine what the pests are and how to treat them.

The best treatment for internal and external parasites is a good prevention-control attitude. If a dog becomes infested with parasites, it is not enough to provide medical attention. All areas that the dog inhabits must be cleaned thoroughly with soap and water and attacked with a proper pesticide. Disinfect all locations where the dog might have acquired fleas, ticks, etcetera, and use the strongest solution possible for kennels and dog houses. Clean out the corners of the house where the dog lies around, and disinfect his sheets, blankets, and other equipment. Spraying the house, furniture, carpets, baseboards, floorboards, crevices, and cracks is necessary to prevent reinfestation. Fleas and ticks and their eggs are tenacious and very difficult to eliminate. In some instances, a professional exterminator is necessary.

Fleas

Fleas live off the blood of the host animal. They can drive the host to distraction with the itching they cause and with their constant, irritating bites for the purpose of drawing blood. They cause anemia and often are the carriers of tapeworm. Fleas can also cause typhus, bubonic plague, rabbit fever, and chronic nonspecific dermatitis (sometimes diagnosed as eczema). Additionally, the fleabites often cause inflammation of the skin, hair loss, and, in some cases, allergic reactions to the bite. Flea infestation is a serious matter.

Fleas are small insects, brown or black in color, wingless, and rapid-moving. They live in the coat of the dog they have infested. Fleas can be found in nearly all parts of your dog's body, but they prefer the neck, tail, head, and chest. One variety prefers the ears and their rims. A favorite hiding place is between the dog's toes and under the tail.

The life span of this difficult pest is one year. Its eggs hatch into larval stages, remaining in the environment up to 300 days. The cycle begins anew when the larvae become adults. Treatment involves interrupting the life cycle and killing off the fleas that have already hatched.

Symptoms of flea infestation are frantic scratching and nipping with the front teeth deep into the coat. A flea-ridden dog often chases his tail, rubs his back on the ground, and even whimpers as he scratches. At these moments the fleas are biting into the skin, taking a blood meal, and moving to another location.

Solving the problem of flea infestation involves treating the dog's environment, indoors and outdoors. Spray or dust his sleeping area with flea-killing products. Next, kill the fleas on the dog's body. Give the dog a bath using a safe flea shampoo or dip. Use a flea collar or douse the dog with flea powder or spray until the situation is under control. The daily use of a flea comb will help determine the progress of the treatment.

Apply insecticide once a week for three weeks in the shrubs and grass where your dog spends time. Inside your home spray deep into the crevices and bedding where your pet sleeps. Spray your carpets and get rid of the vacuum cleaner bags after each use. Flea eggs and larvae thrive in such bags.

The most important aspect of flea control is ridding the dog's environment of fleas as well as treating the dog. Doing one without the other is ineffective. Consult a veterinarian and an exterminator.

Ticks

Ticks are parasites classified as arachnids (spiders, mites, etc.), not as insects. Blood loss and anemia are the potential consequences when ticks attach themselves to a dog's body. The greatest danger from tickbites is the transmission of debilitating and life-threatening diseases. Ticks are carriers of Rocky Mountain spotted fever, tropical canine pancytopenia, and Lyme disease (Lyme borreliosis). Some dogs become temporarily paralyzed from a tickbite (tick paralysis).

The most common ticks feeding on dogs are the brown dog tick (distributed worldwide) and the American dog tick (found throughout North America but most commonly along the East Coast). Another variety is the deer tick, one of the carriers of Lyme disease (found in the Northeast and Midwest). In California Lyme disease is transmitted by the western black-legged tick.

Brown dog ticks establish themselves indoors and in kennels (in cracks, bedding, carpeting, and walls). They can infect dogs at all times of the year. Wood ticks infect dogs only in their adult stage and remain in fields and wooded areas.

The life cycle of a tick consists of four stages: an egg stage, a six-legged larva stage, an eight-legged nymph stage, and an eight-legged adult stage.

Ticks jump onto dogs outdoors in warm weather and may live up to a year in each stage. If a brown dog tick infestation exists in your house, an exterminator will be needed to remove the ticks. If the grounds surrounding your house are infested, cut and remove tall growths and have an exterminator or gardener spray or dust with an appropriate pesticide.

Care of the infected dog involves removal of the tick by killing it with an alcohol-soaked cotton swab and pulling it off with tweezers (usually a small male tick exists alongside an engorged female). It is potentially harmful to burn a tick off your dog's body with matches or kerosene. Dispose of the tick in a container of alcohol or flush it.

Some ticks may be removed by hand, using your thumb and forefinger. However, this is not recommended, considering the possibility of transmission to humans of dangerous diseases such as Rocky Mountain spotted fever and Lyme disease. It is safest to remove ticks with tweezers, forceps, gloves, or a sheet of plastic wrap to avoid contamination of the fingers. A good flea-and-tick dip is an effective means of killing and removing ticks from the dog's body.

Ticks attach themselves to the skin of the dog and feed on its blood. The dog becomes injured by the irritation of tickbites and the loss of blood. When a tick is pulled away from the dog's skin after it has become attached, a small amount of tissue will also be pulled away.

This causes a blood smear and sometimes a swelling. An antiseptic or antibacterial medication applied topically is important to prevent infection. The effects from some ticks can produce fever, paralysis, and even death. Some tick diseases can be transmitted to humans.

If your dog is bitten by a tick, consult a veterinarian about transmitted diseases in your region, particularly Lyme disease. Check your dog's body as well as your own frequently for tick infestation.

Mites

Mites are tiny parasites, barely visible to the naked eye. They are classified as arachnids (spiders, ticks, etc.), rather than as insects and cause serious medical problems and torment for dogs.

Whenever your puppy or dog keeps pawing at its ears or has an apparent inflammation of the ear, it is safe to suspect an ear mite infection. These common, parasitic organisms are barely visible but do move quite a bit, and can be seen by the trained professional. Ear mites are minute white objects seen moving through a mixture of ear wax and dried blood. To rid an infected dog, it is essential that they be diagnosed and treated by a veterinarian.

Two other types of mite cause sarcoptic mange and demodectic mange, which are serious skin conditions also requiring veterinary treatment.

Sarcoptic mange causes intense itching, hair loss, and skin eruption.

Demodectic mange does not cause itching but is indicated by hair loss around the head and front legs and reddened, scaly skin.

These unsightly and uncomfortable skin diseases must be treated for the sake of the dog and its family. Sarcoptic mange is contagious to humans but in a very limited form. It can live only three weeks on the human body but will reappear if the dog is not treated. Demodectic mange is a serious ailment for dogs. However, it is not contagious to humans.

Treatment of all mites requires a veterinarian, whose instructions must be carried out faithfully.

CHAPTER TWELVE

Medical Problems Common to the Golden Retriever

Sadly, there are several diseases and medical defects that afflict some individual Golden Retrievers at birth and are passed on genetically from generation to generation. The following medical conditions are common among Golden Retrievers, although they are seen in many other breeds as well. They are presented here as an aid to the prospective puppy buyer and are also offered as important medical information for those who already live with a Golden.

Individual dogs with a predisposition for most of the following inherited diseases and conditions should be excluded from breeding programs and never mated. Neutering afflicted males and females removes the defects of those individual dogs from the gene pool of the breed and is an important consideration.

Cataracts

Golden Retrievers have a predisposition to developing cataracts. Cataracts are a clouding of the lens of the eye or its surrounding transparent membrane that obstructs light and vision itself. Any spot found on the lens that is opaque, no matter what the size, is considered a cataract and appears as white flecks in the eye or as a milky or bluish white cast to the lens. Dogs of any age can develop cataracts. The majority are seen in dogs under the age of five years. Cataracts are either hereditary or nonhereditary. It is impossible to tell the difference by examining the lens.

Checking into the history of an individual dog's line can more accurately determine the possibility of hereditary cataracts than a physical examination can. However, as cataracts also develop in dogs with diabetes, it is important to rule out medical problems as a cause.

Dogs past the age of eight years usually have some degree of haziness in the lens. Opaqueness does not necessarily mean that a dog is blind. Some loss of visual acuity is due to the light not having the lens to focus on. A cataract is important only if vision is impaired. Congenital cataracts generally do not progress to blindness. If sight is lost, it can be corrected if the cataract is removed. Cataract surgery is not recommended until visual impairment affects the dog's ability to get around.

Dogs found to be free of hereditary eye disease by a board-certified veterinary ophthalmologist can be registered with the Canine Eye Registration Foundation (CERF). Puppy buyers should ask for a CERF clearance for the sire and dam. In 1974 the Canine Eye Registration Foundation was established. One of its functions is to collect data concerning various inherited canine eye diseases. For further information write to V.M.D.B.–C.E.R.F., South Campus Courts, Building A, Purdue University, West Lafayette, Indiana 47906.

Central Progressive Retinal Atrophy
(PRA)

This condition is an inherited retinal degeneration disorder common to Golden Retrievers as well as several other breeds. It is seen in two forms, *central* and *general.* Central PRA is similar to general PRA in its effects on the pigment cells of the retina. However, central PRA additionally destroys the deepest layer of the retina, causing severe vision problems for the dog, impairing its ability to see anything or anyone remaining stationary. Objects that move can still be seen with the peripheral retina. Other signs are night blindness, clinging to owners, and reluctance to climb stairs. Night blindness eventually progresses to loss of day vision and, ultimately, to complete blindness. This condition is thought to be hereditary and, therefore, passed on in breeding. There is no known cure at this time.

When acquiring a Golden Retriever puppy ask for a CERF clearance to avoid eye diseases such as central PRA. See Cataracts above.

Elbow Dysplasia

Elbow dysplasia is found in several breeds of dogs, including the Golden Retriever, and is thought to be inherited. The condition is caused by a failure of the bones involving the elbows to unite and move properly or by bone fragments within the joint. All aspects of this condition will produce degenerative joint disease over a period of time. Fragments of bones or cartilage in the elbow joint are abrasive, causing severe irritation. This results in pain and impairment of the dog's movement.

The first signs may appear as early as four months of age. Permanent or recurring lameness in the front legs may result. The elbow will be thrown out of place as the dog walks or runs. In this condition a dog will hold its elbow away from the chest.

Diagnosis is by X-ray. Surgical removal of the bone fragments will relieve the pain and discomfort, but since the process is degenerative, it may not be halted.

Prevention is the most important way to deal with elbow dysplasia. Concerned breeders try to eliminate the disease from their line of dogs by maintaining accurate records; they do not mate dysplastic dogs, which are removed from their breeding program.

The Orthopedic Foundation for Animals (OFA) in 1990 established a registry service for dogs free of elbow dysplasia in addition to their registry for dogs free of hip dysplasia. For a specified fee the OFA's panel of radiologists will review and evaluate properly taken X-rays of dogs before they are used for breeding. If the dog is found to be free of elbow dysplasia, they will certify it by issuing a number and a certificate of passing. Further information can be obtained by writing to Orthopedic Foundation for Animals, Inc., University of Missouri, Columbia, Missouri 65211.

Hip Dysplasia

Canine hip dysplasia is a complex disease characterized by unstable hip joints and in many cases leads to severe crippling and painful movement. Normally, the "ball" at the top of the thigh bone (femur) fits tightly into the socket (acetabulum) of the hip bone. Hip dysplasia causes these "ball-and-socket" joints to develop abnormally and only loosely fit together in the socket. It is usually complicated by the added presence of osteoarthritis, a degenerative joint disease.

Unfortunately, this debilitating condition is on the rise in the Golden Retriever. It is generally accepted by most authorities that canine hip dysplasia is an inherited condition, even though dogs with no trace of the condition in their line may also produce puppies with hip dysplasia. Some veterinary researchers suspect that puppies with a predisposition for hip dysplasia are seriously affected by accelerated growth, overfeeding, and inappropriate exercise at too early an age.

Signs

This debilitating disease causes lameness with or without pain. Dysplastic dogs are usually born with normal-appearing hips that gradually undergo a progressive structural change. Noticeable signs may appear as early as four months of age. Dysplastic dogs may indicate they are in pain in the hip region, walk with an abnormal or waddling gait, hop when moving quickly, show difficulty trying to stand up, and exhibit a noticeable widening of the hips.

Diagnosis is confirmed by X-ray at twelve months of age, more or less. An X-ray will show the veterinarian the possible presence of degenerative joint disease (osteoarthritis), the shape, contour, and position of the femoral head, and the shape and depth of the acetabulum, the cup-shaped socket in the hipbone. X-ray is essential for an accurate diagnosis.

Treatment

Treatment may consist of surgical or drug therapies or a combination of both. There is no cure for hip dysplasia, but with proper treatment afflicted dogs can live long and healthy lives within the limitations imposed by the disease.

Mild analgesics such as enteric-coated aspirin or buffered aspirin can be used for mild forms of arthritic pain in mild to moderate forms of the disease. Anti-inflammatory drugs (steroids) are given in the more advanced cases in which osteoarthritis is present. Steroids must be used with extreme care and only under a veterinarian's supervision.

Surgery is usually reserved for advanced cases or for those dogs that have not responded to other types of treatment and are in extreme pain. Among the surgical options are *excision arthroplasty* (removal of the ball at the top of the thigh bone), *pelvic rotation* (moving the hip socket to an outward direction, providing more room for the ball of the thigh bone), and *total hip replacement*, which has proven to be the most effective of surgical therapies.

Prevention is the most important way to deal with hip dysplasia. See Elbow Dysplasia, above.

Epilepsy

Epilepsy is a recurrent disorder marked by abnormal electrical rhythms of the central nervous system that induce convulsive seizures in varying degrees of intensity. Golden Retrievers, among other breeds, have a hereditary predisposition to this condition. When epilepsy is an acquired condition, it is usually caused by trauma to the head, resulting in scars on the brain that can lead to seizure activity. Epilepsy can also occur after the onset of encephalitis or any number of viral infections.

Seizure activity originates in the central nervous system. It is caused by abnormal electrical activity in the brain. The effects are seen as abnormal muscular and behavioral actions that the animal is unable to control. Typical epileptic seizures have three phases. The first is an "aura" phase, which is recognizable by restlessness or anxiety. Dogs will sometimes snap at the air or run in uncontrollable circles.

The second phase is the actual seizure itself (the "rigid" phase), of which there are two forms: grand mal, which involves the entire body, and petit mal, which may involve only one part of the body. At the beginning of this phase, the dog starts chewing, head shaking, and foaming at the mouth. The body will go rigid and the dog will lose consciousness. Toward the end of the seizure, the dog engages in paddling movements and may lose bowel and bladder control. Other seizure signs are moaning, screaming, and excessive salivating. The first two phases usually pass within three to five minutes.

Phase three is called the post-seizure state. The dog will have recovered from the seizure but will still be disoriented and wobbly. The third phase may last several hours, giving the impression that the seizure has lasted longer than it actually has. If, during this phase, the dog is stressed by loud noises or too much handling, a second seizure may ensue. Stimuli that can bring on seizure activity are anxiety, fatigue, estrus, fever, loud noises, or overstimulation.

Although epilepsy is a serious medical condition, epileptic seizures are not life-threatening to a dog. Dogs do not swallow their tongue or suffer strokes during a seizure. A seizure may become life-threatening only if it lasts longer than ten minutes. When a dog has a seizure, it is important to ensure that there are no dangerous objects close by. Observe the strength and duration of the seizure. This will be important information for the veterinarian for treatment of your dog.

Treatment

When a dog is having a seizure, it is important to stand away until it is over. Do not try to restrain the dog or wedge anything into the dog's mouth. Call your veterinarian. He or she will most likely ask you to explain what took place: how long the seizure lasted; the events preceding the seizure; and how many times this has happened. Some vets will want to examine the dog to see if they can determine the cause. Dogs with recurrent seizure disorders cannot be cured of seizure activity. The disorder must be controlled, usually by medication. Your vet will decide on the treatment program according to the information you supply. Treatment is also determined by the dog's breed, age, severity of the seizure, exposure to harmful chemicals, underlying diseases, frequency of seizures and their duration. There are a number of anticonvulsant drugs available for epilepsy. Dilantin, phenobarbital, and primidone are a few widely used medications.

Hypothyroidism (Thyroid Deficiency)

Hypothyroidism is a decreased hormone secretion related to a loss of functioning of the thyroid gland. Dogs afflicted with this disorder continue to gain weight even when their ration of food is reduced.

Signs include a dull coat with some hair loss. The skin eventually thickens and becomes scaly and inflexible.

The effect of hormone deficiency in hypothyroidism is a drastically reduced metabolism. Dogs with this condition are lethargic most of the time because of reduced energy levels and have lower than normal body temperature. Other symptoms are obesity, inconsistent estrous cycles, and lack of sharp mental activity. Diagnosis is based on blood tests. Treatment consists of administering a thyroid hormone substitute. Frequent follow-up visits to the veterinarian are necessary to maintain correct dosage. Treatment is usually required for the life of the dog.

Subvalvular Aortic Stenosis (SAS)

This inherited condition is present at birth and occurs most often in large breeds such as the Golden Retriever. It is a cardiac defect that involves an abnormal narrowing or constriction of the connection between the left ventricle of the heart and the aorta. The condition ranges from mild to severe. There are three forms of aortic stenosis: supravalvular, valvular, and subvalvular.

Subvalvular aortic stenosis, the most common of the three types, limits blood flow from the left ventricle of the heart, causing it to work harder to provide the necessary blood circulation required by the body. The disorder is caused by one or more circular formations of fibrous, scar-like tissue beneath the aortic valve. Although the heart compensates for this abnormality, some affected dogs exhibit an intolerance for exercise. Such dogs will struggle and collapse if pushed into strenuous physical activity. Some affected dogs show few or no signs at all. Congestive heart failure and sudden death in the first three years of life is a distinct possibility in severe cases of SAS.

Suspicion of this condition during a routine veterinary examination of a puppy or young dog is the first phase of diagnosis. The vet will detect a heart murmur during the systolic (contraction) phase of the heartbeat by listening with a stethoscope. The diagnosis is confirmed by X-ray, electrocardiogram, echocardiogram (determining velocity of blood flow), or by measurements of blood pressure within the stricture taken with an intravenous catheter.

Both mild and severe cases of SAS are treated medically as with any other heart patient, with preventive measures involving diet and correction of body chemistry. Treatment of choice for severe cases of SAS is open-heart surgery in an attempt to remove the fibrous tissue causing the constriction.

Pyotraumatic Dermatitis ("Hot Spots")

This bacterial skin disease is also referred to by veterinarians as "acute moist dermatitis." Everyone who has ever owned a Golden Retriever is sure to have seen their dog experience at least one hot spot in its lifetime. A hot spot is a self-induced trauma caused by licking, biting, scratching, or even mutilating a portion of the skin that itches and irritates with almost unbearable intensity. Because of the severity of the unpleasant sensation involved, the dog inflicts painful damage to its own skin.

Signs

Hot spots appear as enlarged, circular bumps on the surface of the skin that painfully exude pus. They can enlarge quickly to one or more inches in diameter, causing unbearable itching. The hair usually sticks to the area around the sore, forming a hardened scab. Some hair loss is inevitable.

Hot spots can develop as quickly as two hours after the first indications but usually appear overnight. These painful lesions can turn up just about anywhere on a dog's body but are most often seen along the lower back and thighs. They occur just before shedding begins or during warm, humid weather when dead hair is trapped next to the skin, causing abrasive rubbing and itching. Dogs with double coats are especially vulnerable. Other important causes are flea infestation, flea allergy dermatitis, ear infections, impacted or infected anal glands, and various other forms of skin irritation.

Treatment

Clip the hair surrounding the hot spot and gently clean the inflamed area with a surgical soap such as Betadine, Oxydex, or diluted hydrogen peroxide two to three times a day. The wound must be kept clean and dry. Topical antibiotics help to reduce the irritation.

Effective nonprescription medications that soothe and heal hot spots are Sulfodene medication and Sulfodene shampoo. These are the only nonprescription hot spot treatments approved by the FDA and are recommended by many veterinarians.

If the dog continues to harm itself by licking and biting at the area, a veterinarian may recommend an *Elizabethan collar*, which is a rolled sheet of cardboard wrapped around the dog's neck that prevents it from getting at the wound. See a veterinarian if your Golden develops hot spots.

Hot spots are common to Golden Retrievers and have little or no bearing on decisions involving breeding or buying such dogs.

Von Willebrand's Disease (vWD)

As the popularity of a breed increases, so do the possibilities for congenital and inherited disorders such as von Willebrand's disease. This "bleeding disease" is similar to hemophilia and has been reported in more than fifty dog breeds but is on the rise in a number of breeds, including the Golden Retriever.

Chronic in nature, vWD is characterized by deficiencies in the blood's clotting factors, causing serious medical problems. The severity of the disease's effects vary from dog to dog, with the mildest forms being much more common. Signs and symptoms include hematomas (bruises), nosebleeds, recurring lameness (from blood in the joints), bleeding from the genitalia, and failure of the blood to clot after minor cuts and surgical procedures. Stillborn puppies and early puppy deaths have been attributed to von Willebrand's disease.

To diagnose the disease, a veterinarian will take blood samples and send them to a laboratory for special testing. Treatment is supportive in nature, including drug therapies and blood transfusions. Consult a veterinarian about avoiding anything that might cause bleeding, such as medications (aspirin, etc.), feeding bones or biscuits, intramuscular injections, closely clipped nails, surgery, internal and external parasites, and potentially abrasive pens or crates.

To reduce the prevalence of von Willebrand's disease in Golden Retrievers, breeders are urged to have their dogs blood-tested. If any of their dogs are determined to be carriers of the disease, they should be removed from their breeding program.

CHAPTER THIRTEEN

Home Medical Care

Get a Vet

When your dog is sick, it's hard to think of all things bright and beautiful. Whether a dog needs emergency treatment, preventive medicine, or home medical care, pet owners will sooner or later need a veterinarian. A puppy should get a medical examination as the first order of business, and that requires selecting a vet even before selecting a dog. Ideally, the new puppy should be examined by his veterinarian before going home for the first time. If you already have a vet, you will be able to do this and know exactly whom to call in the event of an injury or an emergency, when saving time means saving life.

If you are about to become a dog owner for the first time, you can find doctors of veterinary medicine in the yellow pages under "Veterinarians" or "Animal Hospitals." You can also call your local veterinary medical society for referrals.

Most owners accept the recommendation of their dog's breeder or one from their friends. It is important, however, to look for a vet who is close to your home. When considering a veterinarian for your Golden, ask about his or her working hours and if he or she offers emergency care after hours. If not, inquire as to the location of the nearest after-hours emergency care center.

It is important that your first visit be a pleasant one for both you and your puppy. Your vet should want to establish a good working relationship, and you must have full confidence in his or her ability.

Home Medical Kit

It is wise to assemble a home medical kit for simple medical care and emergency first aid. Clearly label your medical supplies and keep them in a closed container. A tackle box makes an ideal first aid kit. It should contain **your veterinarian's name, address, phone number, and a current list of medications given to your dog.**

Medical Tools

scissors
straight-edged for cutting bandage, blunt-tipped for cutting hair away from wounds

tweezers
to remove small objects

forceps
a surgeon's tool with a locking clamp for grasping, compressing, and pulling

pen light

rectal thermometer

Materials

sterile gauze bandage
rolled strips 1, 2, and 3 inches wide

large and small gauze pads
dressings to place over a wound or serve as a compress, 3" by 3" or 4" by 4"

cotton balls
for wiping wounds, for applying ointments, etc.

cotton applicators or swabs
for applying medications, cleaning wounds, etc.

adhesive tape
to hold bandages in place

tongue depressors
to hold mouth open, for makeshift splints

mineral oil
   lubricant
instant cold pack
   to reduce body temperature
instant heat pack
   to provide warmth to the body when necessary

Medicines
hydrogen peroxide, 3 percent solution
   for cleaning cuts and wounds
Bacitracin
   antiseptic, antibacterial skin ointment for cuts, wounds, and burns
antiseptic powder or spray
   for cuts, wounds, or burns difficult to reach or pain-sensitive
eye ointment
   the only antiseptic appropriate for eyes
saline eye wash
   to flush the eyes of debris
styptic powder or other form of coagulant
   to stop bleeding
syrup of ipecac
   to induce vomiting; other products for this purpose are hydrogen peroxide, salt and water paste, mustard powder paste, etc.
Kaopectate
   to stop diarrhea
liquid antacid or **Pepto-Bismol**
   for digestive upset
activated charcoal
   for absorbing toxic substances in the stomach

Taking Your Dog's Temperature

One of the most significant indications of illness is an abnormal temperature reading, and every dog owner should know how to get a reading. A rectal thermometer from any pharmacy will do, although you can get special ones for dogs from a pet supply store or mail-order catalog.

By necessity, all dog temperature readings must be taken rectally. Shake the thermometer down below 99°F. Allow the dog to stand or place him on his side and lift his tail. Smear the tip of the thermometer (the bulb-shaped end) with petroleum jelly. Insert the thermometer into the dog's anus. If the dog is large, the thermometer should be inserted to approximately half its length. Smaller dogs require about one-inch insertion. Leave the thermometer inside for two to three minutes. Do not allow the dog to move while the thermometer is in his body. Most dogs will hold still for this procedure if petted and spoken to in a soft, comforting tone of voice. Do not allow the dog to sit until the thermometer has been removed.

Remove the thermometer and take the reading. The average reading for a normal dog is approximately 102°F. This indicates no fever. Large dogs will run a slightly lower normal temperature at around 99.5°F. Many veterinarians consider fever to start at a reading of 102.6°F. Record the dog's temperature every time it is taken so that it can be given to your vet on request. If the dog is recovering from a serious illness, a complete record of the daily temperature is invaluable for the dog's doctor.

Administering Medication

Pills and tablets

First, tilt the dog's head back. To open his mouth, insert a finger behind the canine teeth. Take the pill between your thumb and index finger and place the pill on the tongue, as far back as possible. Close the dog's mouth and gently stroke his throat to make him swallow. If the dog will not allow you to open his mouth, try putting the pill in a piece of cheese or canned dog food to disguise it. The only way to be certain the dog has ingested his medication is make sure he has eaten all of his food. Coating the pill or tablet with oil or butter is also useful.

Liquid medicine

Purchase a plastic syringe from your pharmacist or veterinarian to make this chore easier. Eyedroppers and spoons can also be used. Fill the syringe or eyedropper with the correct dose of medication. Tilt the dog's head at a 45-degree angle and place the syringe between the molars and the cheek. Holding the cheek closed with your fingers, gently squeeze in the liquid. Sometimes liquids can be mixed into food, but be certain only a small amount of food is used to ensure that the dog gets it all.

Eye medication

When applying eye medication, pull down the lower lid and apply ointment to the inner surface of the eyelid with an applicator. *Do not* touch the eye with the end of the applicator or try to apply the medication into the middle of the eye. This could cause the dog to jerk and result in serious eye injury. Eye drops can be applied directly to the eyeball. Rub the eyelid gently to disperse the medicine. When medicating the eye, never use medications that are outdated or not labeled specifically for ophthalmologic use.

Eye problems should never be neglected with a wait-and-see attitude. If you are treating your dog's eye at home and there is no improvement within twenty-four hours, see a veterinarian immediately. Blindness or severe complications could be the result of waiting too long.

CHAPTER FOURTEEN

The Most-Asked Questions about the Golden Retriever

1. Do Goldens shed?

Yes. They are double-coated and shed seasonally. Males shed once a year and unspayed females shed twice a year; the warmer the climate, the longer the duration. Frequent brushing and warm water baths speed the process. Inside dogs shed more due to artificial lighting.

2. Should I protection-train my Golden?

No. It is against the nature of Goldens to use their teeth against people or growl and snarl and would only produce a confused dog and possibly a fear-biter. Goldens have been known to show great heroism, but strictly in situations in which they perceive danger to their owner.

3. When will my puppy be an adult?

Goldens generally mature after the second year, but certain lines take longer and aren't mature until the third or fourth year. Adult Goldens are notorious for maintaining a playful puppy side throughout their lives.

4. Aren't Goldens just like Labrador Retrievers with long hair?

No. They have certain traits in common for which they've been bred but are a completely different breed. Longtime owners find them to be more sensitive to training techniques and corrections. They are in the top five breeds consistently in obedience competition and are noteworthy for their eye-catching beauty.

5. How long do Goldens live?

Life expectancy of a Golden Retriever is nine to twelve years, with many living much longer.

A Golden Oldie.

6. Do I have to obedience-train my Golden?

No, but it is highly recommended. They become mischievous and willful if not given basic obedience training. Besides, they are fun to train and they love it.

7. Should I show my Golden?

If the dog has show potential, is physically sound, and if you have the time and money to invest, why not? Consult your breeder or professional handler. Study the standard for the breed and don't go into showing to make money from your dog. You won't. It should be a way to have fun and show pride in your beautiful friend.

8. Should I breed my Golden?

Only if you are considering it to improve the breed and have a Golden that is physically sound and has been proved to be a correct type and temperament against others of his breed in competition. Be willing to follow up on all puppies you have bred.

9. Should I spay or neuter my Golden?

If you are not showing in conformation or planning to breed your dog, you should absolutely spay or neuter your dog. It is easier on you and the dog emotionally and physically and will help prevent certain health problems. Consult your veterinarian for details. Spaying or neutering will not make your dog fat or lazy and does not change his or her personality.

10. Doesn't a Golden need a big yard? I live in an apartment and don't think it would be fair to own one.

It would be fair if you were willing to train the dog and provide adequate exercise. Goldens make excellent apartment dwellers.

11. Should I get another Golden to keep my current one company?

Yes and no. Your Golden will adore a new companion. They will both give you years of entertainment and they will thoroughly enjoy being with each other. However, if you get a second dog it should be for you. Be prepared to spend double the time on grooming and exercise as well as double the cost for veterinary care, vaccinations, food, and other unexpected expenses. Most important, be willing to double the time you devote to giving the individual attention every Golden needs and deserves.

12. Are Goldens good with children?

Yes. They are among the best of all breeds with children. But as with any breed, good sense should be used when it comes to child-dog interaction. Puppies and adult dogs should not be left unsupervised with young children. Little puppies will not be able to handle the roughness of ear and tail pulling and could be dropped and injured. The adult dog, however gentle, could accidentally bump and knock down a small child unintentionally.

13. Should I own a Golden?

If you like to walk or hike one day and be a couch potato the next, if you have a sense of humor and love to laugh and be entertained, if you can live with dog hair and own a good vacuum, if you love to get and give attention, if you want to compete in the show ring or just have a companion on your walks, if you do not want a protection dog but want a dog that loves the world, and if you don't mind being adored for a decade, then the Golden is for you.

◆ ◆ ◆

Guide Dog Schools

From *A Guide To Guide Dog Schools* by Ed and Toni Eames, second edition, copyright © 1994 (self-published), with permission.

The three breeds most commonly used [as Guide Dogs] are Labrador Retrievers, Golden Retrievers and German Shepherd Dogs. Most schools train both male and female dogs, all of whom are neutered. Schools obtain their dogs by breeding their own or through purchase or donation. From this stock the schools carefully select the animals they believe can be trained to make the best guides.

At about the age of two months, puppies selected for future guide dog training are placed with families, known as puppy raisers or puppy walkers. These invaluable volunteers are expected to introduce the puppies to a wide variety of experiences, such as interaction with other animals, children and exposure to the noise and confusion of family living. The puppies learn to travel in cars and accompany their raisers in public places as much as possible. In addition these devoted volunteers housebreak the puppies and teach them basic manners. Above all, the puppy raisers provide the tender loving care necessary for proper socialization.

When the young dogs are approximately 14 to 18 months of age, their serious training starts back at the school. Professional instructors who have gone through a thorough apprenticeship program work with the dogs for the next three to six months preparing them for their future work as guides.

Becoming a guide dog is not easy. A guide dog should be physically healthy, intelligent, responsive and friendly. A guide dog should not be fearful, aggressive or hyperactive. From earliest puppyhood dogs are continuously evaluated for their future careers. During the year with the puppy raisers, some dogs show indications they would not be good guides and are rejected for further training. The young dogs brought back to the school are further tested for suitable temperaments before going on for formal training. Throughout the training period, any dog deemed unsuitable is disqualified. The schools usually have more dogs available than the actual number of students coming in for training, so further selection takes place during the matching process.

According to Ed and Toni Eames, "Only half the dogs bred or donated as future guides actually graduate. With a current total of 1,300 graduating, this means a minimum of 1,300 dogs are released as pets."

It is their suggestion that those desiring a Golden Retriever be aware of Guide Dog schools as a source of well-bred puppies and adult dogs that for one reason or another were not suited for that highly specialized work. At this writing there are fourteen American and two Canadian programs that serve as a possible source for an available dog.

A List of Guide Dog Schools

UNITED STATES
Eye Dog Foundation of Arizona (Eye Dog)
Uses German Shepherd Dogs only.
8252 South 15th Avenue
Phoenix, AZ 85041
602-276-0051

(administrative office)
512 North Larchmont Boulevard
Los Angeles, CA 90004

Fidelco Guide Dog Foundation Inc. (Fidelco)
Uses German Shepherd Dogs only.
P.O. Box 142
Bloomfield, CT 06002
203-243-5200
203-243-7215 (fax)

Freedom Guide Dogs (Freedom)
1210 Hardscrabble Road
Cassville, NY 13318
315-822-5132

Guide Dogs of America (GDA)
13445 Glenoaks Boulevard
Sylmar, CA 91342
818-362-5834
818-362-6870 (fax)

Guide Dogs for the Blind, Inc. (Guide Dogs)
P.O. Box 151200
San Rafael, CA 94915-1200
415-499-4000
800-295-4050
415-499-4035 (fax)

Guide Dogs of the Desert, Inc. (GDD)
P.O. Box 1692
Palm Springs, CA 92263
619-329-6257
619-329-2127 (fax)

Guide Dog Foundation for the Blind, Inc. (The Foundation)
371 East Jericho Turnpike
Smithtown, NY 11787-2976
516-265-2121 (N.Y. State)

800-548-4337 (outside N.Y. State)
516-361-5192 (fax)
516-366-4462 (computer bulletin board)

Guiding Eyes for the Blind, Inc. (GEB)
611 Granite Springs Road
Yorktown Heights, NY 10598
914-245-4024
800-942-0149
914-245-1609 (fax)

Kansas Specialty Dog Service (KSDS)
P.O. Box 216, Highway 36
Washington, KS 66968
913-325-2256
913-325-2258 (fax)

Leader Dogs for the Blind (Leader)
1039 South Rochester Road
P.O. Box 5000
Rochester, MI 48307
810-651-9011
810-651-5812 (fax)

Pilot Dogs Inc. (Pilot)
625 West Town St.
Columbus, OH 43215
614-221-6367
614-221-1577 (fax)

The Seeing Eye, Inc. (Seeing Eye)
P.O. Box 375
Morristown, NJ 07963-0375
800-539-4425

Southeastern Guide Dogs Inc. (Southeastern)
4210 77th St., East
Palmetto, FL 34221
813-729-5665
813-729-6646 (fax)

Upstate Guide Dog Association, Inc. (Upstate)
P.O. Box 165
Hamlin, NY 14464
716-964-8815

CANADA
Canadian Guide Dogs for the Blind (CGDB)
P.O. Box 280
4120 Rideau Valley Drive North
Manotick, Ontario
Canada K4M 1A3
613-692-7777
613-692-0650 (fax)

Canine Vision Canada
P.O. Box 907
152 Wilson St.
Oakville, Ontario
Canada L6K 3H2

La Fondation Mira Inc. (Mira)
1820 Rang Nord-Ouest
Sainte-Madeleine QC
Canada J0H 1S2
514-875-6668
514-795-3789 (fax)

ABOUT THE PHOTOGRAPHS

All photographs are by Karen Taylor except where indicated. The dogs (and persons) appearing in the photographs are:

Cover

Puppies, 10 weeks old. Windover's Strawberry Fields (Owner: Donna Lemier) and Windover's Yellow Submarine (Owners: William Hurley and Anne Grundy). Both by Ch. Rheingold Devoe 'E Likes It and Ch. Thornfield Ain't She A Mazin.

Chapter 1

PAGE 3: Puppy, 10 weeks old. Windover's Strawberry Fields by Ch. Rheingold Devoe 'E Likes It and Ch. Thornfield Ain't She A Mazin. Owner: Donna Lemier. PAGE 5: Starburst Show Em Some Magic, CD. Owners: Jim and Karen Taylor. Starburst It's Showtime, CD. Owners: Jim and Bonnie LaHousse. PAGE 7: American / Canadian Ch. Lemier's Sunshine Bear, CDX. Owner: Donna Lemier. PAGE 11: U-CD, American / Canadian Ch. Golden Oaks Knock Em Dead, CD, JH, WC, CGC, Canadian CD, WC. Owner: Carla Retell. PAGE 17: Puppies, 10 weeks old. Windover's Strawberry Fields (Owner: Donna Lemier) and Windover's Yellow Submarine (Owners: William Hurley and Anne Grundy). Both by Ch. Rheingold Devoe 'E Likes It and Ch. Thornfield Ain't She A Mazin. PAGE 23: Sun-Day's Tiger Lili, CD, CGC by American / Canadian Ch. Lemier's Sunshine Bear, CDX, and Meadowpond Glory Days, UD. Owners: Dan and Ann Graham. PAGE 26: American Ch. Empyreal's Perfect Strike, American / Canadian CD by Ch. Faera's Future Classic and Ch. Spicewood Empyreal Tiffany, UD. Owners: Jerome and Linda Grzywacz.

Chapter 2

PAGE 33: Sun-Day's M.V.P., CD, CGC by Ch. Lemier's Sunshine Bear, CDX, and Meadowpond Glory Days, UD. PAGE 33: Starburst Show Em Some Magic, CD, by American / Canadian Ch. Lemier's Sunshine Bear and Off-Shore Spirits N' Soda, CDX. Owners: Jim and Karen Taylor. PAGE 34: Thornfield's Mister Mario, CD, CGC, Level 1 Delta Certified Therapy Dog. Owner-Trainer: Eileen Robinson.

Chapter 3

PAGE 38: Photograph by Mordecai Siegal. PAGE 39: Photograph by Mordecai Siegal. PAGE 43: Kyrie Caerfilly Ngaio, American / Canadian CDX, TD. Owners: Edwin and Marallyn Wight. PAGE 45: Isabeau. Owner: Patty Merritt. PAGE 45: U-CD Chelsea's Indian Strawberry, American / Canadian CDX, NA (Novice Agility). Owners: James Litwin and Mary Ratelle. PAGE 47: Thornfield's Mister Mario, CD, Delta Dog. Owners: Randy and Eileen Robinson. PAGE 50: Sharlow's Irish Sundancer, CD, CGC, TDI with Shanna Bires and owner Neva Sharlow, R.N., O.C.N. Owners: Dan and Neva Sharlow. PAGE 52: Ed and Toni Eames at the mall with their Guide Dogs, Saratoga's Edgecombe Ivy, CGC, CDX, Bermuda CD, along with Jake. Used with permission of Karen Newcombe.

Chapter 4

PAGE 57: Ch. Empyreal's Perfect Strike, American / Canadian CD with Janel Grzywacz. Owners: Jerome and Linda Grzywacz. PAGE 61: Sharlow's Honey Dew, Delta Certified Therapy Dog with owner Neva Sharlow. Owners: Dan and Neva Sharlow. PAGE 64: Starburst Show Em Some Magic, CD, CGC. Owners: Jim and Karen Taylor.

Chapter 5

PAGE 67: Starburst Show Em Some Magic, CD, CGC. Owners: Jim and Karen Taylor. PAGE 71: Starburst Show Em Some Magic, CD, CGC. Owners: Jim and Karen Taylor. PAGE 76: Starburst Show Em Some Magic, CD, CGC. Owners: Jim and Karen Taylor.

Chapter 6

PAGE 87: Stonehedge Gabriella. Owner: Nathan Wade.

Chapter 8

PAGE 102: From left to right — Murphy, Bernie, Mario, Duff, Ngaio, Zachy, Magic, Striker, Honey, Sundance — students of Adele Yunck, owner of Northfield Dog Training, Ann Arbor, Michigan. PAGE 106, 111, 115, 121, 127, 132, 136: Thornfield's Mister Mario, CD, CGC, and Level 1 Delta Certified Therapy Dog. Owner-Trainer: Eileen Robinson.

Chapter 9

PAGE 140: Zachary, Sundance, Magic, and Murphy. Owners: Jim and Karen Taylor. PAGE 142: Starburst It's Showtime, CD, CGC. Owners: Jim and Bonnie LaHousse. PAGE 148: Bennington Hill's Zachary, CDX, CGC, and Starburst Show Em Some Magic, CD, CGC. Owners: Jim and Karen Taylor.

Chapter 10

PAGE 154: U-UDX Chelsea's Chippewa Chief, American / Canadian CDX, U-UDX, CGC. Owners: Valerie Marthaler and Mary Ratelle.

Chapter 14

PAGE 194: Greenwood Go For The Gold, CDX. Owners: Dan and Ann Graham. PAGE 195: Sun-Day's Tiger Lili, CD, CGC. Owners: Dan and Ann Graham.

INDEX